DEEP WATER

Simon True: Real Stories. Real Teens. Real Consequences.

Also in the series:

One Cut by Eve Porinchak

Simon True

DEEP WATER

KATHERINE NICHOLS

SIMON PULSE

NEW YORK LONDON TORONTO SYDNEY NEW DELHI

SIMON PULSE

An imprint of Simon & Schuster Children's Publishing Division

1230 Avenue of the Americas, New York, New York 10020

First Simon Pulse edition May 2017

For information about special discounts for bulk purchases, please contact
Simon & Schuster Special Sales at 1-866-506-1949 or business@simonandschuster.com.

The Simon & Schuster Speakers Bureau can bring authors to your live event. For more information
or to book an event contact the Simon & Schuster Speakers Bureau at 1-866-248-3049 or visit our
website at www.simonspeakers.com.

Cover designed by Sarah Creech

Interior designed by Greg Stadnyk

The text of this book was set in Chaparral Pro.

Manufactured in the United States of America

2 4 6 8 10 9 7 5 3

Library of Congress Cataloging-in-Publication Data

Names: Nichols, Katherine, author.

Title: Deep water / Katherine Nichols.

Description: New York : Simon Pulse, 2017. | Series: Simon true

Identifiers: LCCN 2016048467 (print) | LCCN 2017004733 (eBook) |
ISBN 9781481481076 (hc) | ISBN 9781481481069 (pbk) |
ISBN 9781481481083 (eBook)

Subjects: LCSH: Drug traffic—Mexican-American Border Region—Case studies. |
Drug control—Mexican-American Border Region--Case studies. |
Smuggling--Mexican-American Border Region--Case studies. |
BISAC: JUVENILE NONFICTION / Law & Crime. |
JUVENILE NONFICTION / Social Issues / Drugs, Alcohol, Substance Abuse. |
JUVENILE NONFICTION / Social Issues / Adolescence.

Classification: LCC HV5831.M58 N53 2017 (print) | LCC HV5831.M58 (eBook) |
DDC 363.450972/1—dc23

LC record available at https://lccn.loc.gov/2016048467

WHO'S WHO

CORONADO COMPANY PRINCIPALS

Paul Acree: early partner with Lance Weber, soon bought out (Coronado High School (CHS) class of 1970)

Robert Kent Lahodny: swimmer and class president at Coronado High, led the Thai stick trade (CHS class of 1968)

Edward "Eddie" Randolph Otero: skilled swimmer, water polo player, one of Lance Weber's first recruits (CHS class of 1972)

David Stratton: pseudonym, joined in mid-70s and directed operations for all major shipments (graduate of CHS in the 1960s)

Louis "Lou" Henry Villar: leader, born in 1937, started teaching Spanish at CHS in 1965

Lance Cameron Weber: started the Company, later bought out (CHS class of 1962)

CORONADO COMPANY PLAYERS

Don Kidd: became chief engineer (attended CHS)

Allan "Fuzzy" Maguire: pseudonym, skilled mechanic and technology specialist

Al Sweeney: technology and forgery expert (CHS class of 1972)

Leroy Strimple: support crew (CHS basketball player and former Villar student)

Allen Johnson: support crew, worked with Dave Stratton in Reno area

EXTERNAL SUPPORT

Philip DeMassa: attorney for Villar and others associated with Coronado Company in San Diego

Andrew Willis: accountant for Coronado Company in San Diego, also an investor

Luxana Phaksuwan: supplier of Thai marijuana

"Little Ricky" Bibbero: smuggler and supplier of Thai marijuana

Dan: occasional boat captain

Bambi Merryweather: secretary and assistant to Lou Villar

LAW ENFORCEMENT

Jim Brannigan: prosecutor in Maine, previously worked in San Diego

James "Jim" Conklin: DEA agent in San Diego who led the investigation that shut down the Coronado Company, also dismantled Thai marijuana trade

Robert "Bobby" Dunne: DEA agent in San Diego who first pursued Coronado Company

Raymond Edwards: former Assistant US Attorney who prosecuted Otero, Lahodny, and Villar

Dennis "Denny" Grimaud: Coronado police officer who initially tipped off DEA about illicit activities (CHS class of 1958)

Larry McKinney: DEA agent, worked with Conklin later in case

Ralph Shaw: DEA agent, Bobby Dunne's partner

ADDITIONAL

Mike & Jerry Agnor: contractors in Hilton Head, South Carolina

Kevin McInerney: court-appointed attorney who represented Lou Villar

Jack Palladino: private investigator for Phil DeMassa

Sandra Sutherland: co-investigator with, and wife of, Palladino

Barry Tarlow: attorney who represented Phil DeMassa

Chapter 1

SPRING 1969

EDDIE OTERO STEPPED ONTO THE CORNER OF Seventh Street and D Avenue just as Mr. Lou Villar inched his red-and-silver Corvette into a parking space in front of the Coronado High School campus. No matter how many times Eddie saw the car, he always stopped to gaze at the lines, soak in the color, listen to the sound of the engine, feel the speed of the vehicle while it idled.

Mr. Villar stepped out and ran a hand through his dark hair. He wore a crisp, white button-down shirt with a pen positioned at the edge of the pocket, and a narrow black tie. As usual, a pair of Ray-Ban Wayfarer shades covered his eyes—even on cloudy days. Even inside the classroom.

"Hey, Eddie," Mr. Villar said as he tapped the driver's-side door into place and glided toward the sidewalk. Eddie, nearing the end of his freshman year, was not in any of Mr. Villar's Spanish classes. But they were acquainted through Eddie's involvement in water polo and swimming, sports Mr. Villar had helped coach—along with basketball—since he'd become a teacher at Coronado High School in 1965.

Like other swimmers', Eddie's hair, bleached and wispy from chlorine and salt water and sun, flew in all directions, like a dandelion in the breeze. Not that he ever looked in the mirror. He just found himself jerking his head to the side to move tousled strands out of his eyes. He couldn't even remember the last time he'd visited the barber uptown. But it didn't matter. The school enforced no dress code, just an expected social norm—unless you were a drug addict or a complete dork. A few years earlier kids had come to school as if on their way to a job interview: modest mid-calf-length skirts and sweater sets for the girls, collared dress shirts and short hair for the guys. But that seemed like a generation ago.

As Eddie listened to Mr. Villar encourage him to work harder at swimming and water polo (something about wasting his potential as a capable freshman who could become a team leader), the campus came to life. Students parked their Schwinn beach cruisers against palm trees on Seventh Street; some wrapped cable locks around skinnier trunks, and two or three used the pole of a stop sign, fitting their bikes together like puzzle pieces. A lucky few who drove to school pulled into the remaining empty spaces along the curb on D Avenue and Sixth and Seventh Streets.

Eddie adjusted the backpack slung over one shoulder, hooked a thumb under the strap, and strolled toward the classroom past fellow students gathering on the quad according to well-defined cliques. Constructed in 1922, the original Coronado High School had been torn down. In 1960 the city floated bonds, and a demolition derby of sorts made room for a nondescript midcentury structure painted a faded yellow. Eddie thought it looked like the color of mustard that had dried and crusted on your kitchen counter after about three weeks.

The Coronado Islander mascot—a tiki reminiscent of the figures on Easter Island—stood on the edge of the patio, looking badass. A gift from the class of 1960 (probably mourning the disappearance of their old school), the tiki appeared to be constructed from rough lava rock scooped up after a volcanic eruption. More realistically, someone had probably found it at a street market in Tijuana.

When lunch finally arrived, Eddie was fiddling with a combination he couldn't quite remember when a familiar voice traveled down the open-air hall, echoing off the metal lockers.

"Eddiieee! Oscar's. Right now. Let's go."

Once in a while, Robert Lahodny showed up to say hello to various teachers and visit Lou Villar, his favorite, or eat lunch with Eddie. Despite graduating the year before, nobody minded that Bob, or "Lights," as some called him, wandered around campus whenever he pleased. A former athlete and class president, with dark hair and Steve McQueen-like charisma, Bob had been a good student and yearned for those glory days. He enjoyed the short bursts of recognition that accompanied a stroll across campus. Eddie followed Bob to his car, threw his pack in the backseat, climbed into the passenger's side, and turned on the radio.

"Hey, uh, I only have thirty cents," Eddie mumbled. "Can you spot me lunch?"

"Tell you what: Use that to buy me a gallon of gas on the way, and I'll get your lunch."

They pulled into Oscar's on C Avenue, a few blocks from the high school, and immediately looked around to see who else was there. A waitress approached the car and bent over to write their order on a slip of paper, giving them an excellent view. "So?" she asked.

Eddie paused, trying to slow the process while he gazed down her shirt. "Um, I can't decide. What do you recommend?"

She smirked. "Really?"

Bob shook his head. "Sorry, we'll have the usual."

"Right. I'm new and don't know your 'usual.'"

"Burger, Coke, fries. Two of each."

"Make that three fries," Eddie interjected.

"You got it," she said.

In the bustling lunch scene, Bob and Eddie overheard people talk about meeting at the Long Bar that weekend. Infamous for the ease with which a minor could purchase alcohol, the Long Bar had become the go-to location for parties and even better day-after narratives.

"Wanna go?" Bob asked.

"Definitely," Eddie said, already considering the story he would offer his parents. Benefit of the Long Bar: no carding. Drawback: It was in Mexico. A minor detail, however. The trek to a different country amounted to little more than a half-hour drive, with minimal interference, as long as you didn't breathe on the Border Patrol officer at the threshold to the United States. Tijuana sat, just barely, on the other side of the international border. It felt like California, only not quite.

As the drinking hole's name suggested, the bar itself stretched across the entire interior, facilitating conversation, dancing (on the floor and on the actual bar), and the most uninhibited entertainment a kid from Coronado could conjure.

"Remember last time? Lizzy, man . . ." Eddie drifted. "She was messed up. And when that happens, she shows stuff, you know? Maybe we'll get a flash of boob again."

"You didn't see anything. I was there."

"Did so. Hey, I saw that girl Kathy earlier today, waiting for Mr. Villar." Eddie shook his head and exhaled loudly. For a second Eddie wondered how it would feel to have a girl like that wait for his arrival, giggle at his clever remarks, wrap her arms behind his neck, press against him. "That guy has everything."

"Lou? Yeah, I'm bummed he's leaving."

"Wait. What?"

"He's always been nice to me. Like, genuine. That's why I hang out on campus. My stepfather . . . I don't know. He's always busy anyway. Lou makes time for you. He's like a father, brother, and a friend."

"Yeah, he has a way of making you feel, I don't know, important. Why's he leaving?"

"Not sure. He might stay another year, but I think he's kind of done. He's been a great coach and teacher. Everyone thinks so."

"I heard rumors about him and Kathy."

Bob shrugged. "Probably true."

"Other girls too. Since he lives close to school, he takes them back to his house at lunch to 'study.'"

"I heard they practically beg to be invited over! What's he supposed to do with that? Seriously, would you say no?" Their food arrived, moist and steaming. The boys shoved a handful of French fries into their mouths, chewing while tearing the wrappers from around their burgers in short bursts to avoid burning their fingers.

"Maybe I should be a teacher," said Eddie.

"Don't mean to sound harsh, Eddie, but you actually need to be a good student to become a teacher. Lou's smart."

"I'm smart."

"Buddy, you're a different kind of smart. Good on the street. Not so great at a desk."

"How does a Spanish teacher in his twenties drive a car like that and have a smoking-hot homecoming-court girl waiting around for him? I mean, teachers don't make that much money, do they?"

"Maybe seven or eight thousand dollars a year. Not bad. But I think it's because he likes his students. The teachers at Coronado High School are dedicated. Really. They want to make a difference, and all that."

"So how's Mr. Villar do it?"

Bob shrugged. "Look at him. He could be an actor. Girls love coaches. Plus, he's personable."

Eddie tilted his head. "I'm personable."

"Actually, you are. But sometimes you act like an oaf. A cretin loaded with swimming talent, letting it all go to waste. And you do ridiculous stuff, like stealing a can of tuna during a field trip to a factory. Which I heard was really cat food, by the way. And the teacher made you eat it?"

Eddie laughed. "No comment."

"Just letting the junior high legend live on, huh?"

"Yup!"

Bob created a pile of ketchup and began sliding fries through it. "Lucky you'd left Sacred Heart by then. Your knuckles would've been bleeding for a month after the nuns beat the crap out of them with a ruler."

Mouth full, Eddie said, "I want that." A piece of burger fell to the wrapper in front of him.

"You want what? To go back to Catholic school?"

"Funny. I want what Mr. Villar has. Fast car, lots of pretty girls, style, people who like me."

"Well, you have one of those! Let me tell you something: He has more than that. Something intangible, something nobody can define. Anyway, it all starts with money."

Eddie pushed as much of the burger into his mouth as possible, including the stray piece; a thin streak of ketchup stretched across his cheek. "I know." Almost choking on the food, he gulped from the straw in the soda, swallowed hard, then grabbed another fistful of fries. "I know."

"Or maybe it's the other way around. When you have that

charm and motivation, the money comes to you." Bob moved a bag of fries away from Eddie. "What's that grin? Makes you look like you have some amazing idea."

"I have a million ideas."

"Yeah? Maybe take two or three of them to the classroom some time."

"Nah." Eddie laughed again.

"The thing about Lou is that even if he doesn't have tons of money, he makes it *seem* like he does. Like he was born with it, you know?" Bob finished his Coke, then added, "Hey, want to take the ferry over to the Padres game next weekend?"

Eddie nodded. "Definitely."

"Can you believe the bridge is almost done? Takes a hell of a long time to build two miles over the water."

"We should be the first ones to drive it. Or maybe walk across. Or ride bikes. Take the last ferry, and then come back over the bridge."

"Some club is already doing that. They call themselves the Pomona Park Panthers, I think. So the idea's taken."

"Those jocks?"

"Athletes, Eddie. And class presidents. Good students. Yeah, those guys."

"Whatever. We'll do something better. Like swim across the bay. That'd be gnarly."

"Right. They did that already. Got picked up by the Coast Guard. You didn't hear? It seems the US Navy doesn't appreciate kids swimming in the path of aircraft carriers." Bob wiped his mouth with a napkin. "Come on, lunch is over. You don't need another tardy. I'm watching out for you, man. Speaking of swimming, you going to practice this afternoon?"

Eddie shrugged. "Maybe. There's a swell at North. So maybe surfing."

Bob shook his head. "I don't know what to do with you, Otero. Lou told me to get on you about training." As they climbed back into the car, he turned the plastic crank to lower the window, then spun the volume button on the radio. "Favorite new song."

Almost simultaneously they started singing "Touch Me" with the Doors while Eddie drummed to the beat on the sun-faded dashboard.

I'm gonna love you
Till the stars fall from the sky for you and I.

Bob yelled over the music, "I always thought I'd run into Jim Morrison around town some time." Like Bob and Eddie, the rocker had lived in Coronado.

"Right, like maybe at Marco's Pizza?"

"Or Cora Mart! We'd be, like, 'Jim, what's up? Want some of my Abba Zaba?'" They both laughed before jumping back into the catchy chorus, singing out the open windows until they arrived at school.

As Eddie shuffled into typing class, dropped his backpack to the floor, and eased his large frame into the small seat, his mind began to wander.

"One-minute tests today," said Mr. Valliere, a lithe, elegant man whose smile lit up a radius of forty feet. Students called him

Mr. V. to differentiate him from Mr. Villar, even though they did not resemble each other in the least. "Now, folks, I need to ask you not to *pound* on the keys. We have only so many typewriters, and they cost money. And my budget is gone for the year. So let's see if we can learn to type faster and more accurately with a little *grace*, shall we?"

His fingers poised on the keys, a thought far more interesting than the timed test occurred to Eddie. "Hey," he whispered to Samantha, the girl who sat in front of him. "How much you think these things sell for?"

"We're doing a *test*, Eddie," she said with a glance to the front of the room, but without turning around. "Can you stop talking? Please?"

He rolled his eyes. Girls never gave him the time of day.

Twenty seconds after they started the one-minute test, his paper lurched and wrinkled. The same thing happened to the guy next to him, George something, and Eddie jumped up to help him, using just enough force to get George back on track.

George looked over at Eddie when the test ended. "You didn't have to do that. But thanks."

"No problem. Hey, I have a question. How much does a typewriter cost?" His fingers toyed with the lever that advanced the paper to the next line of typing.

"I don't know. Around a hundred dollars. Maybe more."

"No shit. Seriously?" Minimum wage still hovered around $1.65 an hour. One typewriter represented about a week and a half of work.

His face impassive, George examined the paragraph he had typed.

"Compare your paragraph with the one in the text," Mr. V. said. "Be sure to mark every mistake. You'll want to improve your score in the next round."

"Hey," Eddie persisted. "Another question."

George glanced over at him while still managing to keep his attention on the front of the room. Nobody wanted to irritate Mr. V. Not because he would get upset—well, he might, though his good nature usually prevailed—but because everyone liked him so much.

"If you don't mind, I'd like to hear what Mr. V. is saying. I want an A in this class."

"No danger of that not happening! So . . . is that why you look miserable all the time?"

George's mouth fell open, and Samantha turned around to offer a scolding. "Eddie, leave him alone. Don't you know about his best friend's father, who's practically an uncle to him? He's a Navy pilot, and his plane was *shot down* by the North Vietnamese. The families are, like, in mourning."

"Whoa," Eddie exhaled. "He's dead?"

"The family doesn't know if he's dead or alive," Samantha continued in her self-appointed role of proxy. "They've heard from him once. He's a *prisoner of war*. But nobody knows what's going on. It's a total mystery. Don't you know about the other families? There are six or seven from Coronado. And they're all *heroes*. Not that you would know anything about that," she said finally.

"What is so important back there?" the teacher inquired.

"Sorry, Mr. V.," Samantha said. "We were just talking about Vietnam and our concern for the prisoners of war from Coronado."

"Of course. It's terrible. But we're not going to solve the problems in North Vietnam right this minute, in typing class. So shall we concentrate on the work at hand?"

Samantha nodded. "Yes, Mr. V."

"Sorry," Eddie mumbled under his breath. Vietnam was a huge deal in Coronado. How could it not be? You couldn't turn around in this town or step into the Mexican Village restaurant without bumping into a four-star admiral. You couldn't go to sleep or wake up without hearing F-4s landing on North Island, which covered two-thirds of the peninsula and was considered the birthplace of naval aviation.

"I thought you said your father was in the military," George whispered.

"Right," Eddie said loudly enough for the teacher to turn toward them. His father had a job on the base, but wasn't actually in the Navy. Nothing to be ashamed of, Eddie convinced himself. Work meant paychecks—something he wanted and had not yet managed. But it was easy to get intimidated by all the kids of high-ranking officers in this town.

"Less talking, Mr. Otero," Mr. V. said, his patience starting to wane. "More typing."

Eddie's last class of the day was, mercifully, ceramics. In the studio he settled onto the stool and began kicking the pottery wheel. He enjoyed the feel of wet clay seeping through his fingers; this class relaxed him, particularly when he spotted the admiring glances that other students directed toward his latest project.

The art teacher stopped and watched Eddie's motions, pulled her hair back into a long ponytail, then made one gentle correction by pushing on Eddie's thumb to form a more dramatic concave shape in the center.

"Nice work, Eddie," she said. "Did I tell you that the vase on display in the front office is up for another award? You have a real eye for design and balance."

"Thanks." Eddie didn't care about awards with his ceramics. Making each piece helped him feel calm and focused. And his favorite part of the process was giving away the finished pieces to family and friends. He liked the surprise he saw when the recipient realized the kid with the broad shoulders and goofy grin and disheveled hair had created something so intricate, useful, and attractive.

"You might be able to turn this into a business one day," she added.

"Hmm," he said, letting the idea hang for a second before releasing it as an impossibility. The pottery wheel probably wouldn't provide a business platform, he knew, but it always sparked ideas. And with each passing minute, he shaped and stored the information he had learned in typing class for future use—just in case.

Chapter 2

SUMMER 1969

WHEN CONSTRUCTION OF THE SAN DIEGO–
Coronado Bridge finally ended, Bob and Eddie rode their bikes
to hang out and watch the opening day festivities.

Away from the crowd, they let their bikes fall, sat beside
them in the hard-packed sand under the section of bridge that
sloped down to connect with Coronado, and pulled out the cans
of Budweiser they had stuffed into the pockets of their shorts.
Nearby, Miss Bunny MacKenzie's preschool class squirmed
while parents attempted to organize a picture in front of the last
official ferryboat ride. Governor Ronald Reagan, his slick, dark
hair and gray suit in sharp contrast, spoke into a microphone
about construction and progress and free enterprise and the
strength of democracy, smiling and waving to the crowd. Navy
airplanes soared overhead. A barge prepared to launch fireworks.

"Sure changes 'Nado, doesn't it?" Bob mused. "Twenty

thousand people living in our own little bubble. Until now."

"It'll be nice to drive to the Padres games though," said Eddie. "I mean, it would be—if I had a car."

"Yeah, a license would help too! I don't know . . . things will be easier. I guess."

"It does feel different though."

"Like we just got trailer-hitched to the rest of the world."

Painted blue and arched enough for aircraft carriers to pass beneath, the two-mile long structure made Coronado feel like an island, a concept everyone perpetuated. But unlike the Hawaiian Islands, where it was appropriate to say, "He lived on Maui for a year," only unlocals asked, "Do you live *on* Coronado?" Rather, you lived *in* Coronado. Because it didn't take a rocket scientist to see Coronado, which you could circumnavigate with an eight-mile run or cruise around on your bike without ever putting your hands on the handlebars (excluding the two military bases, of course), had an isthmus linking it to Imperial Beach—otherwise known as IB or, in less flattering conversation, Venereal Beach. On a cloudless night from Coronado, you could see the seven or eight miles to IB and beyond to the bullring in Tijuana, Mexico.

Coronado was its own remarkable, isolated, privileged world, yet nobody here was really rich. A few people owned (relatively) palatial homes on Ocean Boulevard. Even so, most students rode bikes to school or drove beat-up cars. Before the bridge was finished, nobody cared where you lived.

Now Third and Fourth, where the bridge entered and exited Coronado, divided the town, making it challenging to cross those streets at certain times of the day—an odd phenomenon for a place with one traffic light. Ocean Boulevard lined the beach side of the alphabetical and numerical grid, and First Street fronted San Diego Bay.

At the center resided a civilian population. These residents had grown up here, circled back later in life, or never left. Some had ties to Coronado through earlier generations that had settled via connections to the Spreckels sugar empire, the construction industry that started with the Hotel del Coronado, or the military, which surrounded the peninsula. North Island Naval Air Station was located on one end, and the Naval Amphibious Base, where SEAL teams trained, was on the other. People liked to call Coronado a sleepy town. But underneath you could sense the uncertainty of war and cultural change and the persistent rumble of the armed forces that belied the town's resortlike allure. And now the bridge hurled everything into the modern era—way too soon for many locals.

Bob sat up. "Did I tell you about my plans?"

"College? Sports? A new business? Marriage?"

"College, for sure. But I'm sailing first. You know I've been down at the yacht club almost every day, right?"

"Where are you going?"

"I'll show you. Are we done with all this stuff? I want another beverage. Let's go back to my house."

"What about the fireworks?"

"We can see them from the road. And my room upstairs."

They pushed their bikes through the sand toward the golf

course, now filling with spectators. Left foot on the pedal, Eddie used his right leg to propel his bike enough to throw his leg over the seat, then rode across the manicured greens toward Glorietta Boulevard. Along the way he skidded through a few sand traps, for good measure. Just as the sky lit up with red and blue and white lights celebrating the new connection to San Diego, Bob and Eddie rode down the middle of Glorietta, arms folded across their chests, balancing on their slow-moving bicycles.

Bob gestured to the endless line of cars. "Told you there'd be no parking. We're already getting invaded!"

They lifted themselves out of their seats, pumping their legs up the Tenth Street hill to Adella Avenue, and dropped their bikes on a bed of monkey tails—tree pod droppings—piled on the front lawn. Inside the house built in 1910 by a ship's captain and designed to resemble a vessel, Bob scanned the contents of the refrigerator. "No beer. How about something more exotic?"

"Like what?"

"A friend of mine worked at the Luau Room at the Del when I was in high school." Everyone referred to the Hotel del Coronado as the Del. "They should have roasted pigs in the ground, but instead turned it into a hoity-toity place. Anyway, he gave me the recipes for their drinks. Are you up for a shark's tooth cocktail? One and a half ounces of Tanduay rum, which we happen to have right here." Bob opened a cabinet and made a grand gesture. "One ounce of lemon juice and passion fruit, though I like to kick up the passion fruit to about two ounces, plus a half ounce of sloe gin."

"Cheers."

"My mom and stepfather are down at the fireworks, so we have the house to ourselves."

Eddie's tone turned romantic, with a sarcastic flair. "What are you saying?"

Bob shook his head. "It's a good thing everyone likes you, Otero. Because you're pretty damn weird." Bob mixed the drinks in his parents' highball glasses, then walked up the wooden staircase. The second floor opened to a large open space comprised of one master suite and a small maid's quarters with its own spiral staircase to the kitchen, like true servants' quarters. It could have been a spectacular house, but it sagged in disrepair.

Posters of schooners and racing boats decorated the walls in Bob's room; swimming medals hung from the top of a lamp. A basketball sat in the corner near a green-and-white Coronado High School letterman's jacket. Bob crouched on the floor and unfurled a nautical map entitled *Oceania*.

"You have a boat?" Eddie asked.

"Working on it. Look . . ." Bob traced his finger from Coronado to Hawaii, then down to French Polynesia, through the Cook Islands, Fiji, Samoa, Palau, the Philippines, and the South China Sea. "This is how I'm starting. And I've always wanted to go to Thailand, so that will definitely happen."

"Yeah, you can get massages every day."

"I think it would be amazing to see the palaces, the ancient ruins, the beaches some people say are even better than Coronado—though I'm not sure I believe it. I heard it's really spiritual, too. Buddhism and all that. I think it might be good for me. Help me figure out what to do. I'm like Dustin Hoffman in *The Graduate*."

"Wait. You're having sex with someone's mom?"

"Yeah, well. Except for that. Whatever, man."

"How long will you be gone?" Eddie didn't want to admit that he would miss Bob.

"I don't know. It's a journey. Still trying to figure out who's going with me and how I'm going to pay for it. Pretty cool, huh?"

In a wistful tone Eddie muttered, "Wish I could go."

Bob shrugged. "Maybe someday we'll have some exotic adventures together, rowing our dinghy onto foreign shores, met by topless girls in grass skirts carrying leis and drinks in coconuts."

"Hey, buddy, it all starts with money."

Bob laughed. "Who told you that crap? There's so much more to life. Unfortunately, you need some cash to understand what that is! Catch-twenty-two, or whatever they call it when you're basically screwed."

They clicked their glasses and tilted them back before Bob rolled up the map.

"Let's ride over to Oscar's and find out where the party is tonight," said Eddie.

"I heard there's something better." Bob paused for effect. "Bike race."

"Bike and barf!"

Little more than crowded, drunken rides, the bike races had assumed the stature of suburban legend. Usually the escapades included hundreds of kids—most of them underage—riding from house to house, stopping for a drink in each location. Sometimes parents were out of town; occasionally moms and dads helped blend margaritas or facilitated access to a tap they'd installed. Members of the stalwart cocktail generation saw little harm in a few drinks among friends, especially when driving wasn't involved. Nobody could get killed riding a bike, after all. Rather than battling the tradition, Coronado Police Department officers were known to block traffic for the mass of riders weaving from one house to another. At the end of the night, the worst tragedies involved skinned knees, bad breath, and unwelcome visitors on living room couches around town.

"Perfect way to finish the night." Eddie and Bob pushed on the pedals to gain speed. "Do we know where they're starting?"

"No," Bob hollered back over his shoulder. "But it shouldn't take too long to figure out!"

Chapter 3

1971

EDDIE FOUND A JOB COLLECTING TRASH ALONG Coronado Beach. Surfing, fishing, and now this gave him plenty of opportunities to observe the lifeguards. The job (lifeguarding, not trash collecting) struck him as an exciting way to make money and meet girls, so he gathered information about tryouts as soon as he turned seventeen at the end of his junior year.

The tests included written components, swimming in the ocean and pool—though covering five hundred meters in ten minutes barely raised his heart rate—carrying someone out of the surf, CPR, and first aid. Soon he found himself in the wooden lifeguard tower at Central Beach, called "Center," binoculars pressed to his eyes, scanning the sunbathers on a vast stretch of pristine sand.

From this vantage point Eddie could see Navy SEALs conducting stealth drills from an IBS (inflatable boat, small) at South

Beach. They moved just outside the break in front of the Hotel del Coronado, about a half mile away from where he stood. He gazed at the Del, the sprawling red-and-white Victorian hotel where movie stars, royalty, and United States presidents had visited since its construction in 1887. People still remembered watching Marilyn Monroe pose for photos while shooting *Some Like it Hot*. The previous September, President Richard Nixon had hosted a state dinner in the Crown Room in honor of Mexico's President Gustavo Diaz Ordaz, with Governor Ronald Reagan and former president Lyndon Johnson. Influential and glamorous people were always wandering the halls. But at its core, the Del was a local hangout.

Eddie noticed the regular beachgoers riding royal blue surf mats in the whitewash: grandmothers in their fifties and sixties outfitted in one-piece bathing suits and rubber bathing caps secured with chin straps. Most of them paid for memberships to use the Del's recreation facilities, including the tennis courts and pool, and frequented the adjacent patch of beach. Eddie liked to check up on the ladies and make sure they didn't need help. They never did though.

The Navy SEALs barely made a splash as they swam along the coast. The water was cold today—maybe fifty-seven degrees. And they wore nothing but those standard-issue tan swim trunks, fins, masks, and snorkels. Watching them train made him think again of the never-ending Vietnam War, the draft, and the year remaining until his eighteenth birthday.

The radio crackled with Russ Elwell's voice. "Hey, yeah, Eddie, we got another stingray. Get the pan ready."

Elwell's experience as a lifeguard on Coronado Beach since 1952 earned him the honorary title of admiral. Because the lifeguards referred to their leader as captain—hinting at some semblance of military hierarchy—the nickname informally elevated him above anyone's actual job.

"Ten-four." Eddie climbed down the ladder leaning against the side of the tower, jumping past the last few rungs into the sand. A nearly completed, more permanent brick tower stood right behind the wooden structure, almost ready for the lifeguards to transfer their headquarters. The guards kept a metal folding chair nearby so they could help stingray victims who didn't know to shuffle their feet in shallow water, a technique that alerted the rays, nestled and invisible in the sand, to oncoming traffic. Rays did not appreciate getting stepped on. So when an innocent bather accidentally put his weight on the slim animal, its long tail shot up, full of barbs and venom, immediately transforming the beachgoer into a hobbling, weeping victim who needed to soak his abused foot in hot water.

It was such a drag when it happened to guys, Eddie thought. But he liked helping the girls and never judged their halting tears. He'd been stung after jumping from his surfboard and could verify that it hurt like a son of a bitch.

The Admiral pulled up in the Willys military surplus jeep to deliver a man in his forties, grimacing and holding his leg as though someone were cutting it off with a dull pocket knife, and Eddie began filling the pan just as two new arrivals situated themselves outside the designated jeep area at the tower, which the guards called the "kiddie corral." This prized location was usually full of attractive girls—many of whom showed up at the beach with homemade sandwiches for the lifeguards.

When the two girls Eddie had just spotted turned around on their hands and knees to apply baby oil and brush the sand from their towels (not in the right order, he noticed), Eddie followed their movements, pouring the last bit of steaming water onto the man's leg. "Ow!" he yelped.

"Sorry," Eddie said. "I'll be right back. Hang in there. You're tough," Eddie added, though he didn't mean it. The guy was acting like a baby and should've stuck to building sand castles or throwing a Frisbee.

"Hey," Eddie said to the girls, adopting a casual tone.

"Hi," the brunette said. "Are you a lifeguard?"

"Yep. Can I help you?"

"Really? You look young."

"He's cute," added the one with a hint of red in her long hair. "He looks like a . . . what are those things called? Like an angel, with chubby cheeks. You know what I mean?"

"A cherub."

Eddie let his grin expand.

"A cross between a cherub and the Cheshire cat, I think, with an adorable dimple on his chin," she said.

Eddie touched the distinguishing cleft. "Like Kirk Douglas."

They giggled. "Want to go out tonight?"

"In Mexico?"

"What? We can't go to Mexico! Why not here, on the island?"

Eddie knew they were from out of town. Even so, he didn't want to embarrass himself by getting carded. The drinking age in Mexico was eighteen, or a tip, or a smile. Nobody cared. But things could get more difficult here—depending on the night, the bartender, the location. "How about a party instead?"

"Where?"

"Not sure yet. Have to check with the Admiral. He's our social director. Maybe fishbowl margaritas in Old Town? Or sometimes we do barbecues. Or a bike and barf around town! We could loan you bikes. . . ."

The girls' attention strayed when they saw Mark, a fit lifeguard with dark, curly hair, stepping out of the jeep. They flipped their hair until strands stuck to their gleaming shoulders and refused to move.

Eddie persisted: "Want to see me rip a San Diego phone book in half?"

"Um . . . why?"

"For fun. And because it's hard to do. Only bodybuilders can do it. And me, of course."

"No, that's okay. . . ."

"Eddie! Get over here." The Admiral stood with his hands on his hips, his pectoral and trapezius muscles skipping with every word. "There's a rip coming up at G," he said, referring to the beach at the end of G Avenue. "I saw some kids out there. Take the jeep and move the swimmers south. I'll watch it from the tower."

Eddie liked the Admiral, even though standing next to him made Eddie feel self-conscious about his own lack of definition.

He wasn't fat, just a little soft for someone so active. But Eddie couldn't help it. If he burned five thousand calories, his body screamed for six thousand.

A lifeguard, bodybuilder, world traveler, teacher, and some-time actor who had managed to land bit parts alongside the likes of Elvis Presley and other megastars since the 1950s, the Admiral had taught Eddie how to tear the phone book, a novelty party trick. The Admiral could reduce the three-inch-thick tome into quarters. Eddie loved performing for an audience, who always thought the source of his ability was strength. But the real secret was technique.

Soon Eddie converged with Mark and another guard, Larry, at the area in front of G Avenue to watch the rip current bend and blossom. They used a bullhorn to instruct the swimmers to exit the water and walk south on the beach a few hundred yards to avoid danger. But two stragglers, a young boy and girl, concerned Eddie. Especially since they were facing shore, with their backs to the surf. You only turned your back on the ocean when you didn't know better.

The guards preferred to stay low-key, avoiding scenes that disrupted the California idyll, so they never went in for a rescue without good reason. Eddie hopped out of his jeep to prep while Mark watched and communicated with the Admiral on the radio. Eddie secured the strap over one shoulder and across his body, and held the rope to the oblong, red foam buoy to make sure he didn't trip over it if he needed to run. His other hand gripped the fins. Then he watched.

Standing in waist-deep water, the two kids heard the repeated instructions and began moving toward the beach. But instead of walking, as they'd been told, they tried to swim. Within seconds the current pulled them straight out to the lineup of breaking waves. The radio hissed, "Go."

Eddie launched himself, running full blast as far as he could into the water, where he quickly submerged and slipped into his Duck Feet fins. The one place he felt totally at ease was in—or on—the ocean. That's why surfers made the best lifeguards. Reading the waves and currents came instinctively. Eddie knew exactly when to dive under, fight through, relax and let the current take him. His astrological sign was Cancer, after all. The crab. Omnivores that worked together to provide for, and protect, their families. They also used their thick exoskeletons and claws to advantage. Some even had walking legs that flattened into swimming paddles, which Eddie always thought would've come in handy.

Eddie stroked with his head above water to track the rapid movement of the kids. He arrived at the boy and reassured him. "I got you." Eddie handed him the red buoy and looked around for the girl. "What's your name?"

"Scotty." The boy's lips chattered, causing him to utter his name as three syllables.

"How old are you?"

"Nine."

"Don't worry, Scotty. We'll get you in, no problem. But you have to hang on tight to this."

"Dana!" the boy cried.

"Is that your sister?" She had traveled another fifty yards while Eddie secured Scotty. Mark was now heading out to help.

"Tell me what you guys do for fun together, or maybe fight about." The easy exchange seemed to calm the boy, exactly as Eddie had intended.

"She uses my baseball mitt."

"Can she play better than you?"

"No. I don't know. Maybe."

"Let's get her," Eddie said. "You ready?"

Eddie pumped his legs and took twenty hard strokes, muscles burning with the extra weight. In less than a minute, the two guards had secured both children.

"Good work, Eddie," gasped Mark, who had been a top swimmer on the Coronado High School swim team. "You're *on* today."

"Thanks," Eddie said. They began to move the kids parallel to the beach, out of the rip current, before bringing them through the surf.

A crowd gathered. When Eddie and Mark arrived onshore, a woman ran up with a hand over her mouth, eyes watering.

"Thank you, thank you," she gasped. "My children . . . I *told* them . . ."

"It's fine," Eddie said. "They're good now. But they should probably stay shallow for a while."

"Yes, of course. How can I thank you all?"

"No need. Really."

"I . . . I . . . everyone likes my chocolate chip cookies. Maybe

I can bring a batch for you and the other lifeguards? I'm so grateful."

"We're just doing our job," Mark said. "Happy to help."

"But we won't say no to cookies!" Eddie added.

After tracking the rip current along the beach for a couple of hours, Eddie remembered the girls he had met earlier in the kiddie corral, but when he returned to the tower, their towels were gone. Too bad they missed his post-rescue glow. The Admiral still hadn't told him the social plans for the night, so in the end, it probably didn't matter.

That evening, still flush with saltwater bravura, Eddie hopped on his bike and rode to North Beach, looking to verify rumors of a party. If that didn't pan out, he'd swing by a couple of houses, or maybe Oscar's. People rarely called each other with plans. Why would they? If you had a life, you never stayed home. Plus, your parents might answer the telephone, and that was just awkward. You listened to the chatter before class started, or passed people in the halls and connected conversations that never quite finished, or heard from other lifeguards, or cruised around town to the usual spots. You figured it out.

By the time Eddie arrived and leaned his bike against the rocks along Ocean Boulevard, about a dozen people sat around a fire ring containing something resembling embers. "You call this a bonfire?" Eddie grabbed a piece of driftwood from the nearby fence and stoked the fire until it looked worthy of the gathering, then sprayed lighter fluid on it. Flames leaped into the air. Sprawled on blankets and slumped in aluminum beach chairs with bare feet buried in the sand and beers propped up on bent knees, a few spectators raised a drink to salute his effort.

Lance Weber sat a few feet back from the edge of the fire ring, watching. After graduating from Coronado High in 1962, he had joined the Navy. When he had escaped the disciplined environment, he followed the path of so many others and returned to Coronado. He called Eddie's name, then tossed him a bottle of Corona beer. "A gift from our neighbors down south."

Eddie flicked the cap with a snapping gesture, sending it into the fire with a spin, then sat down near Lance, feeling the cool sand creep into his Birdwell shorts. "Weber! How come you always have what everyone wants but nobody can ever get?"

"Finesse."

"I thought you were in jail."

"Word gets around." Lance's voice sounded even more high pitched and nasal than usual.

"Ya think?" Eddie sipped his beer and picked at the rubber sole of his flip-flops, which his parents still called zori. "Seriously, where were you?"

"Lompoc. Low security. Federal correctional institution, to be exact. Pseudo prison. For nonviolent offenses. Practically white collar!"

"'Cause you're a nonviolent guy."

"To not hurting people or starting wars." Weber raised his beer. "Peace. All good now."

"So did the guys in prison convince you to grow the 'stache? It's pretty."

"Clever." Lance stroked the blond strands on his upper lip before running a hand through his hair, a shade darker than Eddie's and long enough to cover his ears. "I grew this when I got out. I like to experiment with how long I can make it and still eat."

"I guess you need something to do, because it's kind of dull back here, right?"

"Life is what you make of it. In fact . . ." Lance reached into his pocket and took out two slim rolls. "Want one?"

Eddie laughed. "Nah, I'm good."

"You don't smoke?"

"Not much."

"Suit yourself." Weber struck a match and lit the end, then inhaled slowly. A pungent odor filled the air.

Eddie began to relax. "How much did you pay for this?"

Lance shrugged. "Zero. Gift from a friend." He smiled. "Anyways, I heard you made a rescue today."

"I'm a hero," Eddie laughed. "Just kids who didn't understand the currents."

"You're the master, man."

"Like you and your Porsche engine in the VW bus. Masterful."

"Don't you love the sound of that thing? I think it turns me on more than sex. Want to see what else I built? Come on."

Weber passed the joint to the person sitting next to him. Eddie grabbed another beer and followed Lance to the rocks that separated Ocean Boulevard from the beach. At one time the tide had pushed its way up the fifty yards of soft sand and dunes, necessitating the breakwater.

"*Easy Rider!*" Eddie exclaimed, straddling the low-slung motorcycle, its chrome gleaming in the moonlight. "Let's cruise. Right here on the beach."

"I don't want to get it sandy."

"Seriously? That's no fun."

Lance chuckled as he kicked off his flip-flops, pushed Eddie back, and jumped onto the motorcycle barefoot. He revved the engine, steered toward the trail along the fence separating the beach from North Island Naval Air Station, then turned south along the wet sand at the water's edge. The night air, thick with salt and the scent of seaweed and the imminence of an approaching swell, whipped through their hair. Eddie sat behind Lance, holding his arms out to the side like a kid playing airplane, hollering, "Faster!" But Lance ignored him. His motorcycle, after all, was a work of art, and he would drive it exactly as fast as he thought appropriate at any given moment.

"Let's go to Mexico!" Eddie yelled into the wind. "We'll drive around looking for the best tacos and margaritas and fishing spots."

Lance and Eddie continued conversing in the odd yet acceptable manner that involved saying something that felt profound—as if you were alone on the beach among the remnants of beer and clouds of smoke—but did not require, or yield, an answer from the other person.

Lance slowed the motorcycle, made a U-turn at the Del to avoid the soft sand around the jetty, and stopped the motor to watch the moon rising. "Have you ever seen anything more beautiful? It's flat-out mystical."

Eddie agreed, but in that instant found himself battling the strange feeling that he might be missing out on something—life, love, adventure—as though forced to sit just outside where he should be, unable to see the whole picture. He climbed off the motorcycle and walked into the water. The cold pressed on his ankles. To him, the sea was the baby blanket that comforted a distraught two-year-old, the one thing he could not live without. The ocean always looked the same to people who didn't really understand it. But Eddie could see and smell something different every day.

When Eddie wandered back, Lance asked, "You interested in making a little extra money?"

Eddie took a sip of beer. "What do you mean by a little extra?" It had to be worth the effort.

"How's a thousand sound? Give or take."

Eddie choked, circulating the beer through his nasal passages. "Pesos?"

"You're a character. No, dollars."

A thousand dollars? In the time it took for Lance to utter the word "dollars," Eddie saw himself moving from the outside of everything to the very center. "For what?"

"Nothing more than a workout, man. And I hear you're even stronger in the ocean than you are in the pool. So bring your goggles and surf shorts. And fins. Want to know the best part?"

Eddie nodded.

"It's fun." Lance smiled and jerked his head sideways. "Let's go."

Trying to maintain his composure, Eddie said, "Give me a second to throw this away." He jogged toward a large aluminum trash can halfway up the beach. With a deep breath, he suppressed his desire to ask ten more questions. He had just discovered that he could earn one-sixth of his father's annual salary for a single night of amusement with a friend.

After that, he told himself, did the answers to those questions even matter?

Chapter 4

1971

LANCE PICKED UP EDDIE AT ELEVEN FIFTEEN P.M. and drove him across the border. Behind the Long Bar in Tijuana someone appeared; a shuffle of activity and another short drive followed. A few minutes later Eddie stood shirtless and shoeless, armed with instructions, goggles, and fins. Under his arm he tucked a large package that weighed about twenty-five pounds. He trotted toward the water on the desolate beach. When he looked back, the car had slipped away.

A dry breeze raised the fine hair on his arms; Santa Ana winds from inland regions, unfurling toward the coast, often caused ocean temperatures to drop. For Eddie, the impending cold and currents only added to the thrill of swimming in the ocean at night.

His inherent lazy streak ended the minute he neared the ocean or sensed danger and high stakes. The greater the peril, the more Eddie's senses tingled. Lance had not told him what he was carrying, but Lance's history made it fairly simple to deduce. Anyway, Eddie decided to prove his value first and ask questions later.

He squinted, straining to see movement in any direction. Solitude meant safety. But being alone was not Eddie's preferred state. He liked people. In fact, the prospect of this much money made him think about throwing an epic party for all his friends.

He closed his eyes and listened to the whitewater thump and soar, knowing the churning taking place underneath, waiting to hear how the ocean would treat him.

A rumbling in his stomach unsettled him. He wasn't used to swimming at this hour, and the empty sensation made him feel fast but weak, like his whole body might stop working and sink into oblivion before he reached the destination. Yet it never happened that way. Once he found a rhythm in the water, he could go forever. Besides, at swim practice he trained wearing two swimsuits, T-shirts, women's pantyhose, and anything else that might create resistance, so he was used to it. And compared to carrying a flailing victim? The package was much lighter and way less cumbersome.

It took only a few more steps before he felt the sand become hard. But on the sixth, searing pain shot through his right foot. He grimaced as he steadied himself to determine the culprit. Moonlight confirmed what he felt: the moist stickiness of blood. He fingered the jagged piece of glass, with the remnants of a Corona sticker, impaled in his arch. It occurred to him that sitting down would be a bad idea, so he secured one ankle against the opposite knee to gain enough leverage to dislodge the sharp intruder. Well, he thought, if he loved risk, blood in the ocean at night would enhance the buzz. He wiped his hands on the shorts and kept moving.

The wind shifted, bringing the stench of seaweed mingled with a hint of something dead—maybe a marine mammal's carcass. Eddie hoped the animal wasn't right in his swimming path. He'd seen that before. Nasty.

He waded into the whitewash, forcing himself to ignore the sting of salt water seeping into the gash on his foot. He ran his fingers along a rope—a marine surplus bungee cord—attached to the large package. Sealed and waterproof, it contained enough air to float. He slipped the end of the cord around his ankle, in the spirit of the new surfboard leashes, spit into his goggles to keep them from fogging, and dove under the next wave. His heart threatened his ribs before lodging in his throat; he turned his head to the side at exactly the wrong instant, inhaling what felt like a tsunami, which dictated a break to tread water and cough until he could find air again. *Amateur,* he scolded himself. He swallowed, set his course on the lights in the distance, and put his entire body into the next few strokes, making sure he felt a heavy tug on his ankle.

A shadow darker than the night entered his peripheral vision. He felt the presence of something and froze, opening his eyes wide to see ahead and behind. He didn't exhale. Six seconds. Nine. A sea lion poked its head above the surface, snorted through flared nostrils, then disappeared. Why was every little thing throwing him off? At this rate he'd never make it on time. The point-to-point distance wasn't much. But going out far enough to avoid detection, and landing well beyond the border meant swimming a couple of miles. At least.

He reminded himself that a true waterman's fear of the ocean was rooted in respect that never dissolved into panic.

When he started moving again, he vowed not to stop until he caught a wave into his home country. Occasionally he lifted his head to check the landmark that helped guide him. His cadence settled. Underwater he listened for sounds other than the splash of an arm piercing the surface, feeling his fingers ripple with the force of each pull. He spotted the faint outline of the bullring near the international border. An image of his family, hanging out in their kitchen across from Spreckels Park, wandered through his mind. A flicker of guilt followed. He wanted his parents and siblings to be proud of him. Maybe, if he became successful enough, they would be. He could take care of them, make sure they had everything they needed if they got sick or lost their jobs. He would be there to help. The story formed like the clay on his ceramics wheel, taking shape under his fingers, brightening with color and glaze, encompassing people and places he never before imagined.

His navigation skills, honed from years of surfing and swimming in the ocean, led him to a deserted stretch of Imperial Beach that everyone called the Sloughs, pronounced "slews." Outside the break he watched for the flashlight signal to make sure he was in the right place as he read the timing and pattern of the surf, which he judged to be over eight feet. He waited until he felt the familiar lift before initiating quick strokes. With one arm outstretched, he moved sideways along the face. Thick and heavy, the wave closed out and slammed Eddie into the ocean floor, and sent the package bobbing past him until he felt a yank on his leg—like a speedboat pulling him off a dock from a rope tied to his ankle. The pressure disappeared. He cursed himself. Low tide. An unfamiliar surf break. Stupid.

He came up through the foam, gasping, and tore off the goggles now covering everything but his eyes. His head darted back and forth. No bundle. A burst of eggbeater kick—a water polo trick that required an opposite rotation in each leg and a lot of strength, and could put him out of the water above his waist— gave him the vantage he needed. He spotted the dark package, which seemed to have escaped the waves, because it was, by some bizarre force of nature, behind him.

Another wave ascended, seemingly out of nowhere. Eddie tried to go under, but its power lifted and pulled him back, a sea monster grabbing his fins. Every motion proved hopeless. Over the falls he went. A strong young man turned rag doll.

The tumble made Eddie dizzy; he came up for air, spitting and blowing his nose, feeling as though he were still underwater ten seconds after he'd reached the surface. Where was the package? Lance wouldn't give him another chance. He closed his eyes and made himself as still as possible, save the minimal motion required of his legs, and felt the current. He opened his eyes and started swimming head-up freestyle in what instinct and experience told him would be the right direction. Soon it came into view, glistening and rolling in the moonlight. Without moving his head or his gaze, he sprinted, then swam the bundle to shore as though it were a giant water polo ball.

Once on the beach, Eddie fought the urge to lie in the sand and take a nap. Instead, he carried the precious cargo until he reached Lance, who had already returned to the car.

Lance pushed the gas pedal before Eddie even had a chance to close the door. "So? How was it?"

Exhausting. Gnarly. Terrifying. Dark. Really, really dark. And intoxicating. "Fine."

"Pretty hard, right? I've done it." Lance's voice varied in its strangeness. Tonight it sounded like he'd inhaled from a helium balloon but hadn't quite finished the job. "You can see why candidates for this job are . . . how should I say? Scarce."

"I get it."

A few blocks from Eddie's house, Lance stopped and let him out.

Eddie lingered. "So, when do you think I might get paid?"

"When we sell this. Don't worry about it. We can't even meet demand. Stay tuned."

"Right." Eddie threw his T-shirt over a shoulder—after the swim in fifty-eight-degree water, the night air felt warm. As he slipped into the backyard of his family home, a disturbing thought occurred to him. Would Lance swindle him? He pondered this: It was difficult to cheat fellow Coronadoans over the long term. Things caught up with you. There was no escape here. Plus, he convinced himself over the next few minutes, Lance was a decent guy. Not someone who would turn on his friends.

Eddie found himself in the kitchen, grabbing tuna fish, cheese, and mayonnaise from the refrigerator, along with two Hostess Ding Dongs from the freezer. Assembling a double-decker sandwich, he suppressed a laugh, sending another stream of salt water from his nose. This amused him even more.

Because he just realized: If this thing with Lance worked, it could solve all his problems after graduation next year. Yet if someone asked him to do the swim again without getting paid, he probably would. Just for the rush.

Chapter 5

1971–1972

THE MINUTE YOU WOULD DO SOMETHING FOR FREE, Eddie mused, you found yourself getting paid more than you ever thought was possible. Crazy, how the world worked sometimes.

After their midnight run, Lance told Eddie to meet him down by the Chart House restaurant. There he handed Eddie an envelope.

Eddie peered inside. "Just like the movies!"

Lance adjusted his tinted sunglasses. "Never gets old."

Eddie couldn't help himself. His fingers flipped through more bills than he'd ever imagined seeing. This was almost enough for a down payment on a house. "Let's celebrate. I'm buying."

"If you say so."

Walking up the ramp into the Chart House, a mini replica of the Hotel del Coronado perched on stilts over the bay, Eddie turned to Lance. "When can I go again?"

"Next month."

A hostess dressed in a Hawaiian print sundress greeted them. "Hi, Lance! Are you going to the bar, or do you want a table downstairs?"

"Bar, I guess."

"I can take more," Eddie said, already picturing how he would re-engineer the rope system. "A heavier load. Twice as much."

Lance rocked his head from side to side, staring at the line of boats docked at the edge of the bay. "Good to know." His gaze shifted back to the hostess, whose long chestnut hair hung straight down her back, and he broke into a smile. "Really good to know."

Upstairs in the crowded bar, the mood turned convivial. When a waitress approached to take their order, Eddie opened the envelope of cash and removed several one-hundred-dollar bills.

"Wow!" Her tone grew flirtatious. "You buying for everyone?"

"As a matter of fact, I am." He held her gaze. "What's your name?"

"Brittany."

"What time do you get off?"

"Ten."

"What time do you want to get off?" Eddie giggled. "No, seriously, drinks are on me!" A few heads turned.

Lance sighed. "The only problem is that my friend here is seventeen years old. So we'll pretend the drinks are from me. Sound good?"

"Seventeen? Could've fooled me."

Eddie beamed. "So you'll come back?"

"Why don't I work on your orders first? One of everything? Teriyaki steak, lobster, our famous clam chowder? Looks like you can afford it."

"We'll start with artichokes and beers," Lance interjected. "Then the ahi." Lance handed over the wooden slabs that served as menus and turned back to Eddie. "Time to put away the spoils, man. You're making everyone jealous."

Eddie stacked the bills, smelled them, and stuffed them into his pocket; a girl at the bar used her middle finger to dab gloss on her lower lip, watching him. He grinned at her, knowing in one surge of eye contact that his life had just changed forever.

Summer gave way to the crisp mornings of fall and winter, and Eddie's senior year at Coronado High School. His skin retained its bronze hue, and his nose remained pink, peeling, and itchy, which the chlorinated water did not help. He hated pools, but changed his attitude about attending water polo practice every day.

His talent had carried him through his first three years of high school, to a certain extent. But when he jumped in with his varsity peers, Coaches Larry Cartwright and Pike Meade told him an unpleasant truth: Eddie, or Big Ed, as his teammates sometimes called him, had some ability, sure, but nowhere near enough talent to mess around as much as he did. So he decided to make his last year count. He liked swimming fast and feeling muscular, the exhilaration of climbing out of the pool after a hard workout. But he usually loathed the effort it took to attain those benefits. As soon as he finished swatting his teammates with a towel, just wet enough on the end to sting, leave a red mark, and elicit a few swear words from the receiver, he grew bored and wanted to be somewhere else. Not this year though. Despite the subtle layer around his middle—it wasn't much, but he never seemed to replace the insulation with cut abs the way some of his teammates could—he felt as strong as ever. The fraternal atmosphere reminded him of lifeguarding: guys having fun until it was time to come together and get something important done. There was nothing quite like the synergy of a team, when totally different people harnessed their dedication and discipline into one seamless effort.

Walking toward his bike after practice one afternoon, he heard the familiar rumble of Lance's motorcycle. "Hey," Eddie said when Lance cut the motor.

"Where's your shirt?"

"I had to use it for a towel."

"That makes perfect sense. Let's go to the jetty and catch the sunset. Leave your bike. Hop on. I got something for you."

Eddie slid onto the motorcycle, trying not to touch the maroon tie-dyed fabric Lance wore. It looked like an aloha shirt on drugs. They parked between a Ford Mustang and a Torino, and took the long way through the Del to the beach. They navigated the rocks in their flip-flops until they found two flat ones at the end of the jetty.

Lance sat cross-legged in a meditative position. "We have more weed."

"Can you help me out with a fake ID?"

"That's slightly off topic. But yes, my guy in Tijuana can get that done in twenty minutes. Part of our business."

Eddie considered the phrase "our business" as he stared at the Coronado Islands, or Las Islas Coronado. About fifteen miles from the entrance to San Diego Bay, but only eight miles from Mexico, they were part of Baja California—isolated, uninhabited, brimming with fish. He'd already started fantasizing about owning a boat and inviting friends for all-day fishing excursions.

The giant orb, flaming orange and red, slipped into the sea. As the intensity of the brightness faded, the ocean transitioned from windswept to glassy. "So what do you want me to do?"

"Is that Eddie?"

Eddie recognized the voice and turned to see former Coronado High School teacher Lou Villar in paint-splattered dungarees, a Hang Ten T-shirt, and Wayfarer sunglasses, extending a hand. "How are you? Did you graduate?"

"Mr. Villar."

"Lou, my friend. It's always been Lou."

"Just started my senior year. I'm swimming and playing water polo." Eddie didn't know why he felt compelled to impress Lou. It may have been something to do with the fact that the former Spanish teacher looked like Paul Newman in *Butch Cassidy and the Sundance Kid*—one of Eddie's favorite movies. Maybe a bit more rumpled than during his teaching days, but still magnetic.

"Good for you. I'll be sure to catch a few games. You ought to consider swimming more with the Coronado Navy Swim Association. The coach is an Olympic gold medalist, and it's right here in town."

"I'm putting my swimming to good enough use." Eddie and Lance chuckled. "Sorry, Mr. Villar—I mean Lou—do you know Lance Weber? He might've finished before you came to the high school."

"Yeah, we know each other," Lance said, extending his hand. "Met at a party."

Eddie continued. "What are you doing these days? You look like an artist."

"Painting."

"Pictures?"

"Houses."

"Where?"

"All over. Business comes and goes, a little too sporadically, frankly. I left for a little while, with big plans to build a sailboat and explore the world. But that didn't happen, obviously, so I came back. I have a job on Carob Way next week. Ex-Navy SEAL who's now in the reserves. Works as a lawyer during the week, and jumps out of helicopters on weekends. He has an attractive wife who likes to garden and swim." Lou sat on a nearby rock and sighed. "There are worse gigs. Sometimes I wish I'd finished law school. But then I think, *No, it couldn't be any other way.* Destiny, right?"

"I heard you married Kathy."

"Yeah, that was good. Until it wasn't." Lou forced a smile. "We're splitting up. I love her, but I just couldn't limit myself."

"To what?"

"One girl. I thought we had an understanding, but you know how women can be."

No, Eddie thought, he didn't.

"Especially the good ones!" Lou continued. "I open my heart to lots of people, and don't want to be hemmed in like that. Everything comes at a price."

Lance and Eddie nodded as if they understood, but Eddie secretly labeled Lou a fool for letting a girl of Kathy's caliber slip away.

"I'm reading a lot of Carlos Castaneda," Lou continued, "focusing on my spirituality, finding peace, getting rid of stuff. I even traded my Corvette for a VW bus."

"Oh." This struck Eddie as even more idiotic than losing Kathy.

"I'm also studying Transcendental Meditation with Bula again. Bob Lahodny introduced me to it a while ago. There's always a big group at her place. Very engaging conversations about giving up worldly possessions."

"How's that going?" Lance asked knowingly, but Eddie had no idea what they were talking about.

"I don't know." A silence settled between them while they waited for Lou to say something profound about his transformation. "To tell you the truth, it sucks to be poor."

They laughed.

"What are you doing this weekend?" Eddie asked. "Want to go to the bullfights?"

"Why not? Sounds like a perfect escape from all this soul searching."

"You'll have to leave *The Teachings of Don Juan* behind," Lance added. "At least for a few hours."

"I can do that."

"You still live in the same place by the school? Want us to pick you up?" Eddie hoped to wrangle an invitation into the house, where he still pictured a harem of girls lounging on pillows in cheerleading outfits, waiting to address Lou's every desire.

"How about if I meet you guys at Oscar's around two?" Lou stood and stretched his back, watching shades of maroon explode in wild brushstrokes across the sky. "Are you still surfing, Eddie? I have a new nine-six. Actually, it's used and dinged. But it's new to me, and good for a mellow morning at North. If my back isn't killing me from painting all day."

"Definitely. We'll go out some time."

"Catch you guys later." Lou navigated the rocks toward the Del.

South of where they sat, Eddie spotted a group of Navy SEAL trainees heading into the water with an inflatable boat perched on their heads. Lance followed his gaze.

"Those guys are starting a long night," Lance muttered. "Basic Underwater Demolition training. Must be hell week." They watched the small, gray boat push through the surf, almost skimming the surface. At one point the trainees stopped the motor, gripped paddles, and propelled the boat with synchronized strokes and surprising speed before restarting. "Interesting. I wonder how long it takes to inflate and deflate that thing."

"Not long," Eddie said. "Hey, can we do more than once a week?"

Lance stared at the ocean. "There might be a way, but it's hard to say. Joe and I don't communicate."

"Joe who?"

"I don't know. We didn't exchange business cards. I call him Joe the Mexican. My supplier."

"What's the problem?"

"He speaks only Spanish—and I don't. And neither does my occasional associate, Paul Acree. It tends to limit the conversation."

"I speak Spanish. *Quiero un cerveza*."

"I think it's *una cerveza*. Besides, ordering a drink and nachos is a long way from negotiating an international shipment worth thousands of dollars."

"I know that Coronado is Spanish for 'the crowned one.' Or Crown City. Something about a crown."

"There's a lot of guessing and missed opportunities." Lance redirected his gaze to the inflatable boat. "Anyways, we're set for Friday night. About fifty-five pounds. Can you handle that?"

"Sure." Eddie made a mental note to check the surf forecast before pulling that much weight across the border. He'd also have to test his new rig. "What about Lou?"

Lance stood and paused. "What about him?"

"Why not bring him in?" Eddie enjoyed when the dynamic shifted to make him an advisor. "He's a good guy. And it solves the language problem."

"Hm. Not a bad idea, Otero. Let me think about it."

Eddie bowed his head, turned his index fingers into horns, and snorted at Lance as though preparing to charge. "First, the bullfights! Maybe I'll do some shots and climb into the ring. They let people do that, I heard."

"With *training*. You have to take a class, where people hold a set of horns and charge you, pretending to be the bull, so you know what to do. Because when you go in the ring for real, the bulls are real too. Alive, breathing, unpredictable."

"But they're baby bulls! For the novices, I mean."

"Right, they might lick you instead of impale you. You got some cojones. But go for it; I'll be watching."

"I'm starving, and my mom has dinner waiting."

"I'll give you a ride back to your bike. While you're eating, you can think about how we turn our thousands into millions." Lance hopped from one rock to the other, while Eddie paused, absorbing what he'd just heard.

"Millions," he whispered to himself. He broke into a smile and skittered across the rocks to catch up with Lance, knowing, without a doubt, that someday he would be able to call himself a millionaire.

Chapter 6

1972

ASTRIDE HIS MOTORCYCLE THE NEXT MONDAY afternoon, Lance cruised through the Country Club section of Coronado. It was named for the polo fields that covered the area until the 1940s, when minimalist, one-story Palmer-style homes—a foreshadowing of tract housing—began replacing prancing ponies and lively contests. He motored down Cabrillo Avenue and turned right on Carob Way, where he spotted Lou climbing a ladder against a garage near a manicured bed of roses. Two girls, around five years old, raced each other along the sidewalk on their Big Wheels.

"Hey, Lou."

Lou glanced back from his work without breaking his brush-stroke rhythm. "Lance. Good to see you again."

"I was wondering if you'd be interested in helping us out with some work."

"I have two more jobs after this, so I'm kind of busy. Honestly,

I don't need any more work. But thanks for thinking of me."

"One evening, for two or three hours. Fifty bucks. And dinner. And interesting conversation." Lance threw in the last part to appeal to Lou's intellect, which he suspected was more substantial than any of his jobs had ever required.

"Why me?"

"You speak Spanish, right?"

"*Claro*. Born in Havana, and raised there until my family moved to New York in my teens. But I think you knew that."

"So how about a short break in the routine? No obligations after that."

Lou moved the brush up and down six more times without answering, then sighed, "*¿Por qué no?*"

"So that's a yes?"

"Sure, why not?" Lou dipped the brush into the bucket, eased the excess paint from the bristles, and turned back to the garage.

Lou, Lance, and Eddie traveled to Rosarito Beach together. They sat at a round table on an uneven porch outside a modest beach house. Eddie and Lance watched while Lou talked about supply with Joe the Mexican, a burly man with a voice like gravel. They sat at a round table on an uneven porch outside a rented beach shack. Language, culture, and colloquialisms connected Lou and Joe immediately. Eddie saw that Lou was a guy you could bring to a dogfight or a cosmopolitan cocktail reception. Amiable and handsome, he fit in anywhere. Joe invited Lou to sit down for enchiladas and beer, and Eddie watched Lou's body language, mannerisms, and facial expressions, the way he expanded in the chair, opened his legs, and chuckled, mastering the room.

Forty-five minutes later, the three departed. "All set," Lou said. "Twenty-five kilos."

Lance handed Lou fifty dollars on the spot—a full day of work painting houses—and watched Lou's dark eyes sparkle.

"Want to come back next time?" But Lance already knew the answer.

"*¿Por qué no?*" Lou answered. "I have some ideas for you."

After engineering a rig that kept even the heaviest loads connected to him—across his torso—Eddie felt confident, despite the swell. When he arrived, the sloughs were breaking hard: closed-out sets that no human could punch through without feeling like he'd been shoved inside a washing machine. And with fifty-five pounds of deadweight? That tempered even Eddie's daredevil streak.

Thank goodness he was training hard this year with water polo and swimming. He could track his destination without getting tired. And the eggbeater drills had turned his legs into tree trunks.

He started to go in, but a wave broke faster than he expected, grabbed the package, and yanked him until he could reclaim it from the whitewash, using all his strength. He decided to swim out and wait for a lull. But something felt off.

Instinct warned him before he saw the glint of a top fin, probably belonging to a thresher shark, disappearing beneath the surface. He braced himself. Then with the speed of a professional boxer, he punched the water, aiming for the shark's nose. He flailed until he made contact with skin that felt like sandpaper. The shark's massive tail—as tall as its body was long—whipped to the side, scraping Eddie's skin and knocking the wind out of him. A memory of a kickball game in third grade flooded his consciousness. Someone had pummeled him with a line drive when he wasn't looking, sending him to the asphalt, paralyzed until he could gasp and wheeze. From that moment he swore never to be caught unaware. Eddie could tread water holding his breath for four or five minutes, dive to thirty feet, and take two minutes to pry an abalone from a rock with a crow bar. He reminded himself of these abilities while his imagination conjured a chunk of abdomen missing, leaving him deformed, grotesque. He saw himself crawling up the beach, dragging a massive block of grass behind him. He would be shuttled to the hospital, his sins forgiven because of his hideous state, soon appearing on Johnny Carson's show to talk about the harrowing attack.

Bam! A wave crashed and held him under, bringing him back to the reality of his status: unwelcome guest in the shark's home. The distraction had let him drift into the lineup. Contrary to his promise during that humiliating third grade recess, he struggled to find the surface through the foam and roar and discomfort, creating a short circuit in his senses.

When he felt the sand under his feet, he limped to shore. An infusion of stingray venom was all he needed right now, but he didn't have the energy to shuffle. Staggering up the beach, he hoisted the load, ignoring the rocks and thorns under his numb yet somehow highly sensitive feet. Rivulets of blood traveled down his leg among the fine blond hairs. But an examination of the gash revealed a less dramatic truth: a cut from the formidable fin, but little more.

Even so, he mumbled to himself, "There has to be a better way."

For the next meeting with Joe the Mexican, Lou came prepared. The handshake was followed by backslaps. Dressed with the care of his early days in teaching, Lou opened his jacket and presented a contraband Cuban cigar to Joe as one would a diamond to a prospective spouse. Joe passed the cigar under his nostrils and inhaled. Lou eased into the conversation and, at one point, lifted his trademark Wayfarers and leaned toward Joe as though confiding in an old friend.

Off to the side, Lance listened for any hint of a familiar word. But he couldn't track the rapid pace of the conversation, which seemed to have a weightier, more serious air than the last time. He recognized a fundamental shift from the elementary Spanish and miming games that had characterized his earlier deals with Joe the Mexican.

"What just happened?" Eddie mumbled to Lance when Lou and Joe stood and parted ways.

"Something good, I hope."

Lou kept walking past Eddie and Lance, impassive, silent, until they arrived at the Pinto parked at the edge of Rosarito Beach. As Lance started the engine, he turned to Lou, sitting in the passenger's seat. "Well?"

"I just got you a good deal on *one hundred kilos*."

Lance's eyebrows jumped. He reached across Lou to open the glove compartment, smoothed out an old napkin, and started scribbling calculations with a pencil. Lou grabbed the pencil, crossed out Lance's numbers, and wrote new ones. Eddie leaned forward in the backseat to watch, sensing a learning opportunity he rarely identified in school.

Lance looked up at Lou. "Nice work."

"Thank you."

"I have a feeling this is going to cost me more than fifty dollars."

"And you are correct."

"Now . . . how do we move it?"

"I could swim a couple of times in one night," Eddie offered. "Or we could use an inflatable boat. Like the Navy SEALs."

"I've been thinking about the Zodiac too," Lance said. "But that kind of weight in the surf will submerge it. We'll need swimmers to move the load from the beach to the inflatable. But on the other side, we can go all the way in."

A police car cruised behind them and slowed until Lance spotted an acknowledgment from Joe the Mexican, sitting in a rocking chair on the cottage's porch. The car eased past.

Lance began driving north. All three felt compelled to stay silent until they reached the border crossing. An armed guard examined the surfboards, racked on top of Lance's car, and leaned into the driver's-side window to ask if they were carrying anything back into the United States, which always forced them to suppress a laugh. Everyone stashed alcohol in secret compartments and under floorboards, and nobody seemed to care all that much. Still, this was another level, and ever since completing his stint in Lompoc, Lance preferred to avoid taking chances at the border. Your fate rested on the guy who happened to check you and your car, whether or not his wife had yelled at him that morning, or any number of random circumstances.

"No, sir," Lance said.

Once they were speeding up the Strand, Lou said, "I want a cut of the next shipment. A percentage. I'll help."

"You already helped." Lance's voice hit an unsteady high note.

"No," Lou said. "I want *in*. You need me."

"We got this wired. It's pretty easy."

"Nothing ever stays easy," Lou cautioned.

Lance mumbled, "I'll have to talk to my partners about it."

Eddie yelled from the backseat: "I'm good with it."

"Then I'll have to talk to Acree."

"Screw him," Eddie said. "His value just went right out the window. He's no fun anyway."

"You're going about this all wrong," Lou explained. "Lots of trips with small loads. You need more volume and less frequency. Reduce your chances of getting caught. It's all about probabilities."

"Right, okay. If everything goes well with the next delivery, you'll get your share." Even as Lance said the words, forcing his voice to sound deeper and resonate with authority, he sensed a pivotal change in the control over his own operation.

Lance turned on the radio to hear Paul Simon singing:

What your mama saw

It was against the law

He raised his voice over the music, trying to shift the topic to something more general. "Have you ever wondered if weed might become legal? Not with Nixon, obviously. He thinks drugs are 'public enemy number one.' But what if McGovern wins? Or down the road? Think it could happen?"

"Are you kidding?" Lou shook his head. "This 'war on drugs' is not going to stop for a while. They're filling jails with minor, nonviolent offenders. Small-timers."

"They're obsessed with heroin and cocaine," Lance said.

"Yeah, that's so much worse!" Eddie interjected from the backseat. "This stuff's practically harmless."

"I agree," Lou said. "But to many lawmakers, drugs are drugs. So the border's only going to get tighter; the sins that could put someone away will only get smaller. In case I haven't answered your question: No, my friend, some things will *never* be legal."

"Maybe that's better," Lance offered. "People like what someone tells them they can't have."

"I know I do!" Lou said. "We're heading for a recession, too. That'll change the market. When people are stripped of luxuries, they deserve to relax."

"You know a lot about money and stuff?" Eddie asked.

"Economics, my friend. And yes, because it's all intuition." Lou turned to face them. "Do you know anyone who might want some painting gear? Brushes, rollers, pans? Because I'm giving all those worldly possessions away."

Everyone laughed.

"Nah," said Eddie. "I can't think of anyone who would want them."

Chapter 7

1972

WHEN THE AIR SHOULD HAVE BEEN CRISP ENOUGH for a light jacket, another Santa Ana overtook the Coronado High School campus. Eddie liked the dry, hot winds only when he was on the beach. At school, where not a single building was air-conditioned, the weather felt stifling and oppressive. Seniors gathered on the lawn near the science building. Eddie suddenly missed Bob and wondered what exotic activity might be consuming this moment in his South Pacific adventures. Restlessness overwhelmed him. Why was everyone just lying around and complaining?

With a burst of energy, Eddie walked through a dozen or so classmates in a lazy sprawl on the lawn toward the science building, where a long canvas fire hose sat curled up behind glass. For a split second, he thought maybe he shouldn't cause problems in his senior year. But the notion disappeared; he lifted his foot to break the glass, turned the lever, and dragged the hose out the double doors. Then he directed the stream toward his classmates.

Shrieks and hoots soared from the crowd as he began spraying everyone with water. A few girls hollered at him as they ran outside his range and examined their now transparent dresses and shirts. Some stood under the water, raised their hands, and chortled. One girl removed her blouse and started twirling around in her bra, arms outstretched.

Eddie doused everyone until someone stopped the flow. Of course his next stop was the principal's office, where he received a two-day suspension and semilegendary status. He didn't mind; the break would coincide with the next gig.

Twenty-two minutes after the appointed time, Eddie jogged down to the beach to find Lou and Lance trying to pump up their new purchase: an inflatable boat spanning twelve feet from bow to stern.

"That's not how you do it!" Eddie ran toward them. "Hold the valve. Here, I'll show you."

"You're late," Lou said. "And don't shout."

"Sorry."

"We're going both ways in the ocean; precision is important."

"It's not that far."

Lou stopped, leaned close to Eddie in the darkness, and lowered his voice. "I'm well aware of the distance. Don't let it happen again."

Eddie had never seen this taskmaster side of Lou, and it

made him uneasy, as did the sudden realization that Lance knew more about boats and motors than any of them—even Eddie. He should try to keep his mouth shut. And show up early. Rising stakes diminished the clubby feel of the operation—in a hurry. "Maybe we launch the next one from Rosarito," Eddie offered. "That might be easier."

"Maybe," Lou said. "But we're doing this now. So let's focus. Acree's here too. He can help swim everything out through the surf onto the Zodiac."

"Paul?" Eddie groaned. "Why?"

"Eddie, he's part of the team." Lou used his teacher voice, though he didn't want Paul there any more than Eddie did.

The next few minutes of silence and industry revealed an unexpected dynamic: the teacher-turned-entrepreneur, the former inmate with a mastery of boats and engines, and the high school athlete suddenly started working together like a professional team that had honed its practice over many months.

Paul stood off to the side, crossing and uncrossing his arms, waiting to be told what to do. But the other three were too focused to bother with instructions. Eddie didn't like Paul, who had graduated from Coronado High in 1970. Nobody did, really. Paul's greasy hair, lumpy build squeezed into a five-foot-five-inch frame, and nervous silence gave the gregarious Eddie a bad feeling, like going to work with a fellow fireman or lifeguard you worried could not get the job done. Paul could have been nice enough to make up for these flaws; instead, his negativity and sarcasm grated on Eddie. Plus, Eddie suspected that he'd started using drugs heavily, which probably explained everything.

After some fumbling with the new gear, Eddie, Lance, and Paul disappeared into the darkness.

The nose of the boat skittered over the whitewash and cresting waves, occasionally bouncing Eddie and Lance from their seats on the rounded edge, spraying their faces and T-shirts with salt water.

"Never boring!" Eddie shouted.

Lance gunned the motor even more. "Never."

Just outside the surf in Tijuana, Lance idled while Eddie swam in and ran to the shack, kicking up sand behind him. Paul trailed behind, but Eddie did not slow down; he hoped the intensity would discourage Paul.

Joe the Mexican pervaded every deal, along with his personal supply of beer, tequila, tacos, mariachis, and money, but as usual remained completely invisible during an exchange or delivery. Two of Joe's workers (now they were armed, Eddie noticed), nodded at Eddie and Paul before disappearing into the shadows. Apparently everyone was feeling the higher stakes.

Eddie double-checked the waterproof casing around the rectangular bricks, then worked with Paul to place each one in a bag that would float, and swim them through the surf to the Zodiac. When they finished multiple trips, Lance hoisted Paul into the boat while Eddie hooked a leg over the side, pulled himself up, and wriggled back into his T-shirt. They wedged in the last brick, covered the load with a tarp, and lashed it down. Lance pulled the crank with such force that the engine caught the first time. The boat motored into the darkness, sputtering with the weight. But they had not stationed themselves far enough from the beach.

When the moon emerged from behind a cloud, Eddie watched the ocean shift. It happened in seconds. "There's an outside set coming!" He remembered Lou's admonition about the volume of his voice—after the words came out.

One after another, the waves blossomed in front of them as far as Eddie could see. "Faster!"

Lance accelerated. Every lift of the bow was enough to make Eddie reach for some part of the shipment and test the stability. Up each face they went, landing with a thud on the back side.

"Paul! What the hell? Don't just sit there. Make sure we don't lose anything!"

"I'm gonna fall out!" Paul made a halfhearted effort to hold on to one of the ropes. "I'm supposed to organize supply. That's what I do."

"Not anymore," Eddie mumbled.

"I think we made it," Lance said finally.

But another section of water thickened and ascended, a faint glimmer.

Eddie felt a chill pass through him. "Another big one. Way out. Go, go!"

Lance gunned the motor, a string of obscenities unraveling from his mouth, his blond sideburns soaked with salt water and sweat.

The nose of the Zodiac turned up. Eddie could see no hope of salvaging the shipment if the crest of the wave tipped the bow just past vertical, enough to upend the boat and flip it upside down. And unless he and Lance and Paul could escape this monumental back flop, they would be crushed under far more than the wave. If they lived, they would owe Joe the Mexican and his compatriots in a big way. Neither option seemed ideal.

"We won't make it." Lance said. "Punch through!"

Eddie knew that Lance loved to live on the edge as much as he did, and he heard the agitation in Lance's voice. He understood that piercing the liquid wall might not work; they were not riding a thin surfboard, after all. But in that same instant, Eddie threw himself over the blocks, grabbed the rope holding everything in place, and pushed down on the flexible bow in an attempt to slip through just as the lip curled and began to crumple, a slave to gravity.

It worked. But the force tore Eddie from his perch, throwing him into the water with a wrenched shoulder and the sting of rope burn on one hand. Hearing the boat gain distance on him, Eddie started swimming. He wanted to take off his shirt but didn't want it washing ashore later. A detail like this would not have occurred to him a month earlier. Somehow, this felt like progress, even as his shoulder screamed with every stroke.

Beyond the break, Lance circled around and idled, waiting for Eddie to catch him. "Did you have to go so far out?" Eddie said, breathing heavily when he finally reached the boat.

"Yeah, sorry, but that was the biggest set I ever saw down here, and I been in and out of these waters a lot. Also wanted to make sure you didn't get bored." Lance chuckled.

Eddie pulled himself up with the same technique he had used earlier—thick sides meant the boat did not easily accommodate entries on the water—and searched for space to set his feet on the bottom. His soaked shirt made him shiver. "Hey, thanks for the help, Paul."

Paul scowled. "Thought you had it."

Eddie crossed his arms against the cold, which usually didn't bother him, and thought about wet suits. Some day.

Eddie held on to the ropes with both hands as they bumped and floated over the whitecaps. On the American side they spotted Lou's flashlight signal guiding them to the right spot, but carefully assessed the surf before attempting to go in.

"Wait, wait," Eddie said, watching the waves.

"This isn't my first rodeo, Otero."

"Okay, then, show me how it's done."

The wave toppled behind them. "Lay it down!" Eddie yelled.

A roar broke through the sound of the surf as the motor helped the overloaded boat stay ahead of the onslaught of white-wash that threatened to overtake them. Lance leaned over the outboard muttering, "Come on, baby. Come on." He didn't let up, even when they hit the sand.

"The motor!" Eddie cried. They were supposed to ease into shallow water and unload from there.

"Don't worry about it. We'll buy a new one." Sure enough, it sputtered and came to an abrupt stop. Lou ran to meet them, and from there the operation moved forward without a hitch. In less than five minutes they loaded cargo and gear into the back of Lou's VW bus, and sent Paul on his way with obscure promises about the next gig.

Eddie pulled the sliding door and sat on the floor. All three remained silent until the van hit sixty miles per hour on the Strand, when they erupted with high fives. Lou glanced at Lance in the passenger's seat and Eddie in the rearview mirror. "I think great things are ahead, my friends."

"You know what?" Eddie mused. "I think we're going to need a bigger boat."

Lance smiled and ran his fingers over the sides of his mustache, growing stiff from the salt water. "You know what? I think you're right."

Everything changed. Imperceptibly, yet definitively. Maintaining his fitness became even more important to Eddie. The training eased "international events," as he called the shipments, and ocean swimming helped him race well for the Islanders. Water polo and swimming fit together naturally, or more accurately, out of necessity. You couldn't play at a high level in polo without becoming a strong swimmer, which meant competition throughout the school year.

He was busier than ever, yet somehow passing his classes and on course for graduation. It felt like some kind of miracle.

Chapter 8

1972–1973

JUNE GLOOM, AS LOCALS CALLED IT, LAUNCHED THE summer season with an ironic flair. Sometimes it began in May. Either way, it became a damp veil between the end of school and the glorious summer. Characterized by temperatures that stayed cool under the haze of one massive cloud the color of slate, the days stayed that way until early afternoon. It barely resembled California. But when Eddie received his copy of *The Beachcomber* yearbook in the cafeteria, it felt like the sunniest day of the year. He flipped to the picture of the swim team, decked out in Speedos on the bleachers at the Municipal Pool, and the water polo team photo in front of the brick wall. Then he found his senior portrait and suppressed a grin. He was dressed in a coat and tie, and his hair was actually combed, probably thanks to his mother. His ears seemed kind of big, he thought, but overall, he had to admit that he looked pretty good. With his square jaw, slight smile, and faraway look, he might be headed for a career in banking, insurance, or acting. The power of illusion. He'd already secured a full-time lifeguarding job for the summer to supplement his income. Then again, that was the kind of work he would've done for free.

Eddie's graduation ceremony, which had loomed as a major life change for him and his parents (as some things do when it looks like they might not happen), passed as a borderline nonevent. You listened to speeches, walked across a makeshift wooden platform on Cutler Field in front of family members sitting patiently in the bleachers, shook the principal's hand and received your diploma, threw your cap in the air (this seemed sort of absurd to Eddie), and partied all night. And that was the end of your education. Or maybe the beginning.

The weather eased back to its Southern California motif. Full-blown summer had arrived, marked by Fourth of July celebrations in Coronado. The military town went all out. A parade the length of Orange Avenue lubricated everybody's party of the year, with regulars finding their friends and drinking Harvey Wallbangers—orange juice, vodka, and Galliano liqueur—concealed in plastic containers they carried on their bicycles. Military demonstrations with Navy SEALs parachuting into the bay, rough-water swimming and running competitions, and, for Eddie, an endless stream of ocean novices venturing into rip currents, utterly clueless. In the safety of the scorching sand, nubile girls turned ripe and glowing within an hour. Everybody wanted Coronado Beach's fine sand to stick between their toes, and the bridge had made that possible.

The guards finally moved into the new, brick lifeguard tower. It was more solid and less likely to get washed away during an unusually high tide, and the height provided a better vantage. It allowed Eddie to see more boats passing by, which always sparked new possibilities for their operation.

They had decided that driving down to Mexico with the deflated boat in the back of the van would be more efficient. So the crew started hosting barbecues in Rosarito at a rented beach house—a glorified shack, really—in the late afternoons and evenings before each delivery, grilling steak, fish, chicken, and vegetables, and sitting around a makeshift fire ring in the sand until dark. It worked as a facade, helping account for the sudden burst of activity in a slow-moving location. But it also served another purpose: It set the stage for an enjoyable evening together; the uncertainty and anticipation stoked laughter and fellowship.

Then they would pump up the Zodiac and set to work swimming the product through the surf to the boat (farther out, to avoid rogue sets) and delivering it to the other side of the border. Eddie was still the only one who could carry fifty pounds through crashing waves. On one occasion Lou helped them swim. But when it left him sputtering and coughing for ten minutes, he swore he would never do it again.

Everything was fine when they were planning and moving, in proximity to the thrill and the danger. But Eddie didn't like the lulls in activity between runs. And when summer ended, so did lifeguarding—except for occasional weekend work. Plus, he had developed a bad habit of burning through each new payment more quickly than the last.

Long after the idea first occurred to him, and in the middle of a day of boredom and too many beers, he and a friend drove to the Sixth Street side of the Coronado High School campus. They climbed the outdoor staircase, broke a window, and started shuttling typewriters to the side door of the van. Eddie basked in a torrent of adrenaline tumbling all the way to the tips of his fingers and toes, mimicking how he felt when a girl touched him, or someone hugged him after receiving one of his ceramics projects, or when he swam fast, or moved cargo from Mexico.

"That's enough," his friend said. "We're totally exposed. Let's head out."

"One more carry," Eddie insisted.

They heard a noise.

"Someone's coming!" Eddie's friend whispered before disappearing.

Eddie waited. "Nah, it's fine." But he realized he was talking to himself. He shambled toward the door, where he fumbled with the knob and slid out sideways with a typewriter under each arm—right into two Coronado Police officers shining flashlights in his face.

The sudden blindness made him flinch.

"Put those down!"

"Okay. Can I go back in? If I drop them, they'll break."

"Otero? Is that you?"

The alcohol had left Eddie's mouth parched and sticky. Suddenly he felt as if he might vomit. "Um. Yeah."

"I know your dad. What are you doing? Damaging school property? Stealing . . . typewriters? Not doing yourself any favors here." The officer held the door open for Eddie so he could return the machines to their respective desks.

"I know."

"Who's with you?"

"Just me. I swear."

"I don't believe it." He turned to his partner. "Do a perimeter check. Call it in."

"I'll put 'em back." Eddie fought the nausea and dizziness overtaking him.

"Didn't you just graduate? And don't you lifeguard at the beach?"

Eddie nodded.

"You'll need plenty of help to get out of this."

"How'd you know I was here?"

"Anonymous tip."

Eddie considered that he'd told one person too many about the evening activity. He always meant to keep things to himself, but would have to do better.

The damage would take a while to undo, Eddie realized. Despite an inexplicable confidence that he would escape serious consequences, he understood, even in the haze and hum of the evening, the stupidity of his choices.

When he was convicted of burglary in 1973, he endured the

wrath of Lou, who asked repeatedly why Eddie had resorted to stealing—a crime of thugs. And if Eddie was going to insist on getting drunk and doing something so ignorant, did it really need to be at Coronado High School, where everyone knew them? But Eddie didn't have a single answer for Lou.

With the safe return of the typewriters, and letters from respected city employees who cared about Eddie and were willing to vouch for his character and explain that losing his job or spending time in jail would be a hardship and most certainly steer him down the wrong path, Eddie reduced his punishment to community service.

He recognized his dangerous attraction to diversions that guaranteed close calls, and promised to stay away from them.

Well, he told himself, at least he would avoid the half-baked ones.

Chapter 9

1973–1974

TO CELEBRATE EDDIE'S NINETEENTH BIRTHDAY, LOU invited Lance and Eddie over for a party at his modest house tucked into an alley near Coronado High School. A wooden fence, rotten and faded from exposure to salt air, surrounded a condensed grassy area.

Eddie saw other people who had helped with deliveries along the way, as well as former and current students. Most important, the yard and house were filled with girls. Ian Anderson sang and played the flute from the speakers Lou had hooked up to the turntable. On a bookshelf nearby, vinyl albums spanned entire shelves: Eric Clapton and Cream, the Doors, Jethro Tull, Van Morrison. The smell of teriyaki chicken and fresh fish doused in lime and cilantro floated through the yard; surfboards of various lengths leaned against the side of the house. People relaxed in aluminum beach chairs, eating chips and guacamole, wrapping and smoking.

In the kitchen, Eddie opened up cabinets in search of a large bowl and began mixing what everyone called "Eddie's punch."

Lou approached, sipping a glass of wine. "Congratulations on making it through high school. Touch and go there for a while, wasn't it, my friend?"

Eddie laughed as he poured 151-proof Bacardi into the icy red punch sprinkled with fruit. "Yeah. But I always figure it out."

"You do indeed. What do you have there? A little bootleg?"

Eddie shrugged. "Rum we smuggled from Mexico in a friend's spare tire compartment! The rest is my own recipe. Wait till you try it."

"I prefer Bordeaux to Bacardi and . . ." Lou sniffed the concoction. "Whatever this is. Kool-Aid of some sort?"

"Here." Eddie dipped a paper cup into the bowl and offered it, dripping over his fingers, to Lou. "I couldn't find a scoop thing, so . . ."

"A ladle? Maybe next time. I don't want it to ruin my palate."

"Whoa, okay!"

"Eddie, you know I'm just teasing you."

But Eddie could see that the money was doing its work on Lou, transforming him, or as Lou might say, delivering him to what he was meant to be.

A girl with straight brunette hair parted in the middle, flowing around her shoulders and draped across the sundress barely covering the small mounds on her chest, leaned into Lou and gazed up at him. "You said you'd teach me about wine."

"I'll teach you about my punch," Eddie offered. "It's my own recipe. Not like wine, which just comes out of a bottle and is nobody's recipe."

Girls paid more attention to him now, that was for sure. Well, they did when he carried a lot of cash, which seemed to come and go like the Santa Ana winds. But this girl acted like Eddie hadn't said a word. He was invisible when Lou was around. Everyone was—except when Lou directed his attention toward you. In that moment you became the center of the world.

Lou's hair was longer now and a little lighter and curlier, like he'd done something to it at a salon. There was a gold chain that hadn't been there at Coronado High School, along with a thick mustache that altered the clean-cut appearance he'd sported as a teacher. And he was also making time to exercise, because he never carried that extra five or ten pounds around his middle, Eddie noticed, even though he was already in his midthirties, the time in a person's life when most things started to fall apart.

"Meet me in my van out in the alley. I'll be there in twenty minutes." Lou brushed his lips against her ear until her mouth parted and found his.

Eddie stared at the scene, then shook his head. "Really? Over-priced wine and . . . the back of the van? Didn't you have another girl out there an hour ago?"

Lou shrugged. "It's cozy out there. They like it."

"You keep getting older, but they don't."

"What can I say?" Lou wrapped his arm around Eddie's shoulders, and all Eddie's animosity slipped away. "Your time will come, my friend."

Lance wandered into the kitchen and held up a cup for Eddie to fill. "Pure ethanol?"

"Almost," Eddie laughed. "Next time we're doing one-hundred-ninety-proof Everclear."

"I tried that Polish vodka once." Lance's voice squeaked even more after drinking and smoking; his eyes took on a glassy appearance. "Spirytus. Surprisingly mild."

"Maybe that's because you go numb after the first sip," Lou lifted his wineglass. "That's why I prefer something more . . . cultured."

"Everyone's got different goals," Eddie said, watching a familiar face appear in the doorway to the living room. "You know him?"

"One of my favorite former students." Lou raised his voice. "David, come join us! You know Eddie?"

Eddie lifted his chin and said, "I've seen you body surfing at the beach. And you know Bob Lahodny, right?"

Dave nodded. "Yeah, he graduated a year behind me. Bob's a good guy."

"He's my best friend."

"David plays drums for a band," Lou said. "He's creative and meticulous." The fondness in Lou's voice surprised Eddie, as though Lou were talking about his favorite child, even though Dave was only about ten years younger than Lou. "Don't you also play the guitar and piano?"

Dave nodded. "I sing once in a while too."

Lou nodded approvingly, then turned back to Eddie. "David might want to help us out on the beach occasionally."

"Yeah, the band isn't doing so great," Dave offered. "Maybe I shouldn't sing!"

"Any help you need," Lou said. "I think you'll be a great addition."

Eddie watched the exchange with curiosity and uneasiness. But before he could decide what to say, Dave disappeared into the other room, and Lou leaned toward Lance and Eddie with a serious expression. "You guys have a minute?" Not waiting for an answer, Lou carried his wineglass toward the back of the house. They followed.

"You made some improvements to the place," Lance noted. "Silk pillows that match the paintings. That kind of stuff."

"Accents," Lou said, glancing at the new furniture, art, and window coverings that helped him transform the bungalow into something out of a magazine. The VW van would be the next thing to go. But he had to admit it came in handy sometimes.

They closed the door to a room he used as an office, with a cherry wood desk and law books on the narrow shelves, and sat in stiff leather chairs while Lou outlined his reinvestment plans. "We've got a lead on a new supplier: Pepe de Mexicali. If this works out, CapEx will be in order."

"What's that mean?" Eddie asked.

"Capital expenditures. We need to invest in the business and not just run around with all the money. There's potential for a lot more. But we have to hire people to help us off-load, and rent a stash house, maybe in Point Loma."

"And buy bigger boats," Lance suggested.

Lou nodded. "We'll work it out over the next few months."

"Sounds good!" Eddie said, clapping his hands. "Let's do it."

And with that, the board meeting adjourned.

Lance purchased a forty-foot cabin cruiser and a Chris-Craft—with Lou's permission, of course. As he'd done with motorcycles and cars, he rebuilt the engines to meet the needs associated with high surf and heavy loads.

After a large delivery, Lou invited Eddie to meet him at the Chart House for dinner. Eddie arrived early and sat at the bar, slipping the bartender one hundred dollars to serve him a tequila and lime, and a beer.

"Man, you put me in a tough spot, Otero," the bartender grumbled.

"Sorry, Matt. I always make it up to you."

"That you do. Just so I know, you on your bike?"

"Walking."

"Even better." Matt eased the shot glass over to Eddie, who scanned the room before licking salt he'd sprinkled on his hand, tossing the liquid to the back of his throat, and sucking on the lime wedge. He took the beer and sidled over to a blonde. She had a spray of sun-induced freckles across her nose and cheeks. Her friend was even more attractive but still in Eddie's range (a radius that grew significantly with money, he knew). Both had been watching him. He pulled from his pocket a roll of cash the size of a fist and smiled at them.

"Can I buy you girls a drink?"

They stared down at the bundle of bills and dipped their chins flirtatiously. "Sure. Looks like you could take us shopping, too."

"I can do anything. Just tell me what you want."

"Eddie." Lou appeared next to him, pressing on Eddie's elbow—a gentleman's push—to get him to the table. "Shall we sit down?"

When Lou turned, he caught someone watching him. The man appeared to be in his early thirties, with a mustache and dark blond hair, and the stance and build of an athlete. He looked familiar, but Lou couldn't place him. A bar regular at the Chart House? Or maybe the Manhattan Room, another popular watering hole? Then again, there were no strangers in Coronado, which was part of the problem.

Eddie peeled off another hundred, handed it to the bartender, and said to the girls, "I'm having dinner with my friend, but I'll see you later. One of my favorite bands—West Coast Ironworks—is playing uptown later. Ever heard of them?"

"No, but it sounds fun," the blonde said.

"Our friendly neighborhood bartender will take care of you until I'm done with dinner. Right, Matt?"

Matt took the hundred, nodded, and kept wiping the counter.

"Eddie." Lou's tone turned sharp. "Let's have dinner."

Money still in his hands, Eddie followed Lou to the table. The waitress was a new girl with shoulder-length black hair that contrasted with the white dress covered in plumeria flowers. Lou stopped paying attention to Eddie and began asking about the quality of the steak and other items on the menu, which he knew by heart. Grinning, Eddie fanned dozens of hundred-dollar bills across the center of the table. Then he sipped the beer and smiled at the waitress, waiting for the moment when she turned away from his more enticing dinner companion. "I'll have the fresh fish."

"Anything else?" She stared at the cash. "An airplane? A luxury cruise?"

"Maybe," he said. "Want to come?"

The busboy delivered butter and a basket of steaming sourdough and dark brown rye bread. When Eddie dropped a piece of bread to his plate, his fingers tingling from the heat, Lou glanced back at the athletic-looking man, who was now sitting on a stool, leaning against the bar, drink in one hand, watching the whole scene. Lou reached out and scooped up the bills. "May I see your wine list?"

"Sure," the waitress said, throwing another glance at Eddie before turning around.

When she left, Lou lowered his voice. "What the hell are you doing?"

"Bread's hot. So good. You should have some. Butter melts right away."

"That's not what I'm talking about. What are you thinking, waving that much money around? Grow up, Eddie. Try to be a little more . . . understated." Lou covered the bills and looked back at the bar. But the guy had turned around and was talking to his buddies. If other people weren't looking, maybe they'd grown accustomed to Eddie using cash as a place mat.

Eddie folded his arms across his chest and looked around, avoiding eye contact with Lou. Finally he said, "Can I have my money back?"

"Will you keep it in your pocket?"

"Yeah, sorry." Eddie played with his napkin. "You mad at me?"

"No, Eddie. I'm sorry I spoke to you that way. But you need to be more careful."

"But we never have any problems! And didn't you walk into the bank a few days ago with a load of cash and pay off the mortgage on your mom's house?"

Lou sighed. "Yes."

"So how's that different?"

"It's a bank, not a bar. And I don't know. It just is. Now come on, we're supposed to be celebrating. I have plans."

"Like what?"

"I'm going to Hawaii. I think it would be good to lay low for a while."

"Okay." Eddie stuffed the remainder of a large piece of bread in his mouth, then called for the waitress to bring them a steamed artichoke.

Lou gestured to the bar and lowered his voice. "Do you know that guy? On the end, with the blue shirt?"

Eddie looked. "I've seen him around. Used to be a running back on the football team. He ran a ninety-yard kickoff return for a touchdown. Not once, but like, lots of times. Holds a bunch of school records in track. Played basketball, too, I think."

"What's his name?"

"Grimaud. But I don't know which one. Big family. They're all athletes."

"What's he do now?"

"Um . . ." Eddie shrugged. "Not sure."

"Maybe you can ask your bartender friend if he knows."

"He's just a guy having a beer." He waited for Lou to excuse him from the task, but that didn't happen. "Yeah, okay, I'll check it out."

Chapter 10

1973–1974

IN THE NEW DRUG ENFORCEMENT ADMINISTRATION'S San Diego field office, Bobby Dunne stroked his auburn mustache and used the tip of his cowboy boot, scuffed and covered with Mexican-American border dirt, to pull the metal chair over from the next desk so he could sit back and prop up one leg. If there had been a window, he might have gazed out. But he didn't really need to; he knew every signpost and street corner here in National City. The offices were sparsely furnished, heavy with file cabinets whose drawers required a hard yank to open, steel case desks, and an oversize sombrero emblazoned with *Roberto*. The remnant from a party in Tijuana rested on top of a folding table near a coffeemaker, a can of Folgers, a bent spoon (because someone had misplaced the plastic scoop), cream that looked a day or two past viable (only because Dunne shared the area with other agents; he was very particular about fresh cream in his coffee) and C&H Pure Cane Sugar from Hawaii (which he used sparingly). Not that amenities in the office mattered; their jobs required them to be out, cruising undercover, watching through binoculars for suspicious vehicles, blending in, and working informants in bars and on the streets with cash and promises of protection (that they really couldn't guarantee).

None of it rattled Dunne. This was tame compared to his gig in Guadalajara, where he'd learned the bizarre yet stringent rules of street dealers, the layers of corruption inherent in every system. Other guys his size—a lean five feet seven inches—might have considered it a drawback. But Dunne used it to advantage. Everyone tended to underestimate him, and he liked it that way.

Working the early days of a new government organization had its challenges. But he couldn't imagine doing anything else. When he became a state agent in 1965, he considered fighting drugs a noble profession; avaricious dealers were cruel people who cared nothing about kids, and he believed that getting illegal narcotics off the street helped people, made a difference in the world. Every morning when his alarm buzzed at five thirty, these thoughts—no, realities, he corrected himself—pulled him out of bed.

Even though the Nixon administration had pushed for every minor arrest, Dunne and his team set their sights higher. In 1968 he was the first agent in the US to buy one ton of marijuana. Afterward his boss started calling him *One Ton Dunne*. Teasing and swearing were part of the job. Nobody was exempt, so if you couldn't roll with it, you were better off finding another line of work.

He hated the attention and media frenzy that went along with the big busts, but that didn't keep him from acknowledging one bonus from the publicity: His East Coast compatriots chasing established crime syndicates had taken notice when Dunne had nabbed several hundred pounds of marijuana and a few dozen pounds of heroin a couple of months earlier, right after he'd left Mexico and returned to San Diego. Despite the bureaucracy and occasional confusion, Dunne decided that communications with agents in other parts of the country and the all-important Border Patrol were actually improving.

As he refocused on the report in the typewriter, the phone on his partner's desk rang, causing him to hit the wrong key. He muttered to himself and unscrewed the Liquid Paper, which had aged into crusty, stubborn lumps. He pulled out the entire mess to fix the error on the white, yellow, and pink carbon copies.

His partner, Ralph Shaw, called from the other room: "Dunne, can you get that?"

"No!" he shouted back. "I've got this report, and calls, and whatnot. When do we get a secretary?"

"Ah, yeah, maybe when we get air-conditioning."

Dunne had been a cop for several years, but the paperwork for a government agency topped anything he'd ever imagined. It took hours. And if he left in the middle and returned to the task full of new ideas and fresh leads, successful completion of the old business grew more distant and overwhelming.

"How about José?" Dunne spoke fluent Spanish but pronounced

the other agent's name with a hard *J*, like "Joe-say." Some bar joke along the way prompted it, and it stuck. They could never go back. "Can you get it?" Dunne waited. The ringing persisted.

Shaw jogged back into the room, grabbed the phone, then cupped his hand over the receiver. "Guy says he wants to talk to you. See? I'll transfer."

Dunne glanced at the clock on the wall, then back at his tall, thin partner. It had taken them a long time to become friends. But Dunne recognized Shaw's credentials, which included previous stints as a deputy sheriff and a Border Patrol inspector. "We need to leave in five to set up surveillance at the border. I wanted to finish this report." He shook his head and tucked the black receiver against his neck, still trying to peck letters with his forefingers. "Yeah, Dunne here."

"Bob Dunne? Dennis Grimaud, with the Coronado Police Department." He waited. "Everyone calls me Denny."

"Coronado?" Officers in cushy middle-class suburban neighborhoods like Coronado didn't usually have their finger on the pulse of high crime, so Dunne started to tune out the speaker almost immediately.

"Glad your office is up and running," said Grimaud. "Wasn't sure, with that Watergate nonsense."

Dunne saw his partner cover his shiny head—everyone called him *Pelón*, Spanish for "bald"—with a cowboy hat, slip his long arms into a leather jacket, and gesture with a circular motion to wrap up the call. "Listen, Denny, I'm just heading out. You said you got something for us?"

"Yeah. Looks like some kids and a teacher out of Coronado High School have been smuggling drugs from Mexico—swimming them from the bullring to beaches in IB. Might've paddled surfboards, too. Now they're using boats."

Dunne stopped typing. "Swimming? How'd you get this?"

"I graduated in fifty-eight and come from a big family. Here in town, that means plenty of sources. But I also work undercover, and spend time talking to kids on the street. That's how I find out what's going on."

Dunne suspected the understatement meant that Grimaud was a real drug task force guy. He raised a hand to Shaw, a signal that the call had become important enough to delay their departure. "Cocaine and heroin, too?"

"No, just marijuana. Far as I know."

"What have you done about it?"

"I'm always watching. Tried to catch them doing a drop. I heard they landed in front of the Del a few times, but they're elusive. All I've seen is some reckless behavior with money at a bar."

"Which could've come from somewhere else."

"Right. If he sold a house—for cash."

Dunne mumbled to himself.

"And the kid's only nineteen or so," Grimaud continued. "Name's Ed Otero. Graduated from CHS in seventy-two. Convicted of robbery, but got off easy."

"I hear what you're saying, so why does it seem . . . far-fetched?" And it did, even to Dunne, who had worked in the trenches throughout his career. "They sound like amateurs."

"They're kids, mostly. Except for Lou Villar. He came to teach Spanish at the high school in the mid-sixties, after I graduated. I think he's changing the game. They may be amateurs, but they're acting like pros."

"Anything else?"

"There's a boat called the *Lee Max Two*. Roman numbers for the two. Chris-Craft. High end. And very fast."

"Not your average fishing skiff, huh?"

"Maybe for James Bond. Might want to follow up on the registration."

Dunne grabbed a pencil and spilled the Styrofoam cup half-full of cold coffee onto his desk. "Damn."

"What?"

"Nothing." Dunne repeated the name to himself: "*Lee Max*."

"Let's get together; I'll give you everything I have."

"Right," said Dunne. "Meantime, if you hear anything else, give us ring, okay?"

"You got it."

Dunne pushed the button in the cradle to end the call, perched the receiver on his shoulder, and thought. Shaw returned, impatient, and motioned for Dunne to get going.

For a moment Dunne vacillated between jumping up from his desk or following up on the tip while it had his full attention. Part of him wanted to believe this was little more than a rumor from a lily-white town where jaywalking counted as crime, but his instincts told him Denny Grimaud had just handed him something big.

"One more call." When Shaw rolled his eyes, Dunne continued: "And while I'm doing this, can you find the registration for a boat called the *Lee Max Two*?" Dunne flipped through his metal Rolodex, dialed a number, and made a half-hearted attempt to wipe up the spilled coffee with an old napkin while he waited for someone to answer.

The ringing ended. "Coast Guard."

"This is Bobby Dunne over at the Drug Enforcement Administration office in National City. Could you connect me with a radar expert? I have a few questions about what, exactly, you can detect on the water."

EVEN WHEN ABSENT FROM THE ACTIVITY, LOU
left his fingerprints on every detail. So it took a while for Eddie
and Lance to realize that their partner had never returned from
his Hawaiian vacation weeks earlier, and was running the operation from the middle of the Pacific Ocean.

One night in a rented house, while repackaging for distribution,
Eddie chatted with Lance about their missing patriarch. *What's
up with Lou? He's been hard to reach. Why's he still in Honolulu?
With Sylvia? Miranda? Seriously? Who's she? At the Royal Hawaiian
Hotel? Wait, he says he wants to live there? That sounds kind of nuts.
We're not going to let him do this, right? He knows we'll come get him.
You already have tickets? Cool. I've never been to Hawaii.*

When the plane touched down at Honolulu International
Airport, and Eddie first descended the stairs to the tarmac,

he understood why Lou didn't want to leave. Driving along Kalakaua Avenue, Lance moved at about ten miles an hour to take in the surf shops, bars, and girls in bikinis cradling surfboards under their arms. Even two guys who had grown up on the beach found the scene riveting.

They pulled into the porte cochere of the Royal Hawaiian Hotel, otherwise known as the Pink Palace, and turned their keys over to the team who greeted them with pineapple juice, kukui nut lei, and "Aloha!" After checking in, Eddie wandered out to the back lawn, which fronted the ocean, and inhaled the scent of salt water and pikake. How could this part of the Pacific smell and look like a different ocean? Outrigger canoes glided across turquoise water that glistened in the tropical sun. The approaching winter meant a calm South Shore and potentially massive waves on the North Shore. Eddie didn't want to miss surfing at Pipeline and Waimea Bay before he left. That experience would give him a few stories to tell. He turned to re-enter the lobby—more tropical than the Del, but equally grand—to find Lance on the house phone, trying to reach Lou.

"He's not in his room. Come on, let's find him."

From the beach, Eddie glanced at the Spanish-Moorish architecture of the sprawling hotel that opened in 1927, when visitors arrived via steamship. It seemed familiar, probably because he'd seen it in the background whenever he'd been able to catch *Hawaii Five-0* on television. That show almost made him want to become a cop. Almost.

The beach was surprisingly narrow, dotted with pink

umbrellas perched in sand that felt grainy and rough between Eddie's toes. When someone from the hotel staff offered to set up beach chairs and bring them drinks, Eddie beamed. "Sure!"

"No, thanks," Lance answered. "Maybe later." Then he turned to Eddie. "Come on. We only have a couple of days."

They wandered past the beach lounges but didn't see Lou, then found themselves in front of a raised stand under a large, weathered umbrella, stabilized with a pole duct-taped to the wood. Rows of rental surfboards stood behind a Hawaiian-Chinese boy, maybe around Eddie's age, shirtless and muscular, with skin the color of milk chocolate. "You guys wanna take one lesson?" The Pidgin rolled from the beach boy's tongue like a song.

"We're good, thanks." Lance said. "But we're looking for a friend. Kind of compact. He might have a mustache, dark skin by now, and he definitely has a good-looking girl with him."

"Brah, dat could be anykine guys."

Eddie added, "Kind of a kook on the waves, but thinks he's really good?"

"Oh yeah! Dat guy been surfing wit us ev'ry day. Got his girl out couple times too. She rips. He like paddle one outriggah, too, yeah?"

"Canoe surfing?"

"Yeah." The beach boy cocked his chin toward a gentle break.

"What's his name?" Eddie asked. "Lou?"

"Nah."

"C. R.?"

"'Das it. Hey, you guys want boards? He tips good, so no worries. Here." He fetched longboards for Eddie and Lance.

"Mind if we leave our flip-flops here?" Eddie asked, kicking them into the sand that scorched his calloused feet.

"Flip wha? Slippahs, man. Flip-flop is one mainland word. Don even know what you mean." Then he giggled. "Nah, I'm jes messin' wit ya."

"Slippers."

"See?" The beach boy gestured toward a man balancing on a small wave before tumbling into the water. "Chance 'em!"

Lance and Eddie paddled out. The water felt like warm silk against Eddie's skin. The dormant volcano of Diamond Head loomed across Kapiolani Park; an onshore breeze blew warm against his face. Eddie propelled his board easily through the waves, reaching Lou first. "We've missed you, *señor*!"

"What the—?" Lou shouted, then saw Lance. "When I told you where I was, I didn't think you'd really come over, much less find me in the water!"

Eddie extended his arm, bent at the elbow in an arm-wrestling position between a handshake and high five. Lou grabbed it, grinned, and tried to pull Eddie off his board. Both laughed.

Lance eased up and straddled the board, adjusting the shorts he'd worn on the plane. "Lou, we missed you, man."

Lou shrugged. "It's very peaceful here."

"I can see why you want to stay," Eddie said. "But we're here to make sure you don't."

"I've been thinking that maybe I should stop now." He made a sweeping gesture with his hands. "This is all I really need."

"What?" Eddie yelled. "Stop now? We're just getting started! We're partners!"

Lance added, "I got an idea for something even bigger. You heard of a DUKW? It's an amphibious landing craft the military used in World War Two. Thirty-one feet long, with six wheels. It goes right from the water up the beach to the road. It's nuts."

Lou pretended to watch the surf line.

"Have you been to the North Shore?" Eddie asked.

"Miranda likes it here better," Lou said. "It's more . . . civilized."

Lance's eyebrows went up. "Seriously? You're going to play house with *Miranda* in Waikiki, and get old and tedious in your thirties? What kind of life is that?"

"Comfortable." Lou's gold chain caught the sunlight, temporarily blinding them. "Though I will admit that I'm moderately bored."

"Then come on!" Eddie yelled. "Let's hit the North Shore, Trader Vic's, and head back to our awesome lives."

As they waited for the right wave, Lance said, "Lots of news reports about the Vietnam vets coming home addicted. President Nixon won't stop talking about the 'new menace.'"

"What's new about it?" Lou laughed. "I think it's been around in some form or another since biblical times."

"Whatever. Making it seem new is effective."

"True," Lou said. "His war on drugs has landed a lot of small dealers in jail. And the general public seems to be all for it. That's why I wanted to get out of town for a while."

"To the land of *pakalolo*!" Eddie said, using Hawaiian slang while miming the smoking of a joint.

"The government already has the Bureau of Narcotics and Dangerous Drugs, the FBI, the Bureau of Alcohol, Tobacco and Firearms," Lance said. "What more can they do?"

"The DEA—Drug Enforcement Administration has an office opened in San Diego. Or maybe South Bay."

"Nixon's on his way out," Lance said. "So don't worry about it."

Lou paused. "I always feel like someone's watching us. Did you follow up on that guy in the bar, Eddie?"

"Um, yeah, I was going to tell you. But we've been busy, and you weren't around."

"Well, who is he?"

"Dennis Grimaud. People call him Denny."

"And?" Lou asked.

"Uh, he's a cop in Coronado."

"But you already knew that, didn't you? Never mind. Is it worth the risk?"

"Hell, yes!" Eddie hollered. "There's no way he has anything on us. Those guys'll never catch us. And we're *good* at this, man. We can stop whenever we want."

A silence settled between them.

Eddie added: "What else are we gonna do? Punch in at nine? Make eleven grand a year? Die of boredom?"

Lou snorted. "No."

"*So?*"

Lou shielded his eyes against the sun and scanned the beach.

"Okay," he said finally. "But I think I'm done with Coronado."

Eddie spun his board to face Lou again. "Done with Coronado? Where our company is based? It's like . . . we're the Coronado Company!"

"It's too close; everybody's up in your business. Don't worry—you'll never know where I am." Lou added with a touch of sarcasm, "But I'll always know where you are."

"You're starting to sound like a kingpin," Lance said, half joking.

"Come on, my friends." Lou grinned and started paddling. "Let's ride the wave that's under us!"

Lance worked to catch the same one, and Eddie, the most skilled surfer by far, laughed as he dropped in on them. They whooped and tried to move to the front of their boards, hang ten, and maneuver along the small face for as long as the momentum would carry them. Eddie wished someone would take a picture and freeze this moment on an idyllic afternoon in Waikiki, when the three of them had enough money to do whatever they wanted, and they cared about nothing beyond the next adventure.

Chapter 12

1974

INTERNATIONAL POLITICS PERMEATED SMALL-TOWN
life in the form of an ongoing energy crisis. OPEC, the
Organization of Petroleum Exporting Countries—a cartel
launched about thirteen years earlier—exerted its control over
the world's need for oil. Eddie found himself waiting in line at the
gas station on Orange Avenue for ninety minutes or more, and
even then, station owners enforced a limit. Prices had escalated
from thirty cents per gallon to a dollar. The staggering expense,
rationing, and shortage ignited panic. Lines of cars wrapped
around several blocks. Stations often ran out of gas. Unease
pervaded even casual conversations: What if you couldn't get to
work? What if the world became paralyzed?

Lance and Eddie assigned some of the lieutenants they
had recruited for beach off-loading to wait in line, fill up their
cars with less than five gallons, and deliver gas cans with the

remaining allotment to the garage of Eddie's new house, which he had purchased in his mother's name.

When Eddie heard Lance's motorcycle, he lifted the garage door halfway and invited Lance to slip underneath.

"How many boats can we run right now?" Lance asked.

Eddie calculated the supply and the gallons needed in the worst possible conditions, because running out of gas on the ocean at night was perilous enough. With a hold full of illegal narcotics? Flat-out dumb.

Eddie handed Lance a piece of paper with the calculations written in pencil. He knew that with one glance, Lance could assess the amount that Eddie had assigned to each boat.

For some reason, hoarding gas felt much worse to Eddie than importing. Maybe because the gas crisis directly affected people worried about getting to work, afraid of losing their jobs. People he loved. (He made a mental note to buy enough extra gas to help his parents and siblings, just in case.) He saw less harm in supplying people with something they wanted, enjoyed, and shared with friends. That was about recreation, choices.

If he thought too hard about people getting addicted, remorse bubbled to the surface. Then again, this was why the Company stayed away from the more destructive cocaine and heroin. Even so, he rationalized, why should he feel responsible for what other people smoked? He wasn't a drug *dealer*. He wasn't forcing anyone. This was America, after all.

"I think we should stick with the cabin cruiser," Eddie said.

"Agreed," Lance said. "But we should carry a big reserve in

case we have to stay offshore for a while. I've heard rumblings about eyes on us."

Eddie laughed. "They're not moving too quick."

"I have plans to throw them off."

"You want to fill me in?"

"Sun Tzu's *Art of War*."

"Prison wisdom?"

"Pretty much."

Eddie chuckled. "That should do it."

"But gas is the focus now."

"When do you think this'll end? My parents are not happy."

"If your folks run out, you can always share some of your booze with them. That should run a car!"

"What does Lou think?"

"He says the Arab countries think if they push an oil embargo, they can control what we do with Israel. And when a country becomes needy and dependent on places like Saudi Arabia, Iran, and Iraq, it all goes to hell. So it's either going to work, or they'll realize they've lost their biggest customer and come running back to us. He says to me, 'Game theory.' Then he goes on about Nixon, Watergate, Ford, Kissinger, and the 'geopolitical situation.' Anyways, Lou doesn't think gas prices will ever go back to twenty-five cents."

"Jeez, Weber. If I wanted a lecture, I would've called Lou myself."

"Supply and demand! Makes the world spin."

"So we're good if I can add fifty gallons to this supply?"

"Right on."

"What's Lou up to anyway?"

"Lounging in his new Solana Beach digs. Drinking wine with Kerrie, who moved in with him, by the way. Planning vacations around the world. Telling me how we need to tighten up the operation because we have too many cooks in the kitchen. Figuring out a way to make Paul go away. You know, just being Lou."

"The new Lou. With his silk shirts and gold chain and three-hundred-dollar bottles of wine from wherever the hell in France."

"Bordeaux."

"Yeah, sometimes I think he forgets where he came from."

"Maybe he can never forget where he came from, that his dad died when he was three, and maybe that's what drives him. Or maybe he was always an aristocrat, and we just never knew it. Hey, he wanted out, and we went and dragged him back from Waikiki. So I guess we can't complain."

Eddie nodded. "Can't deny we're a damn good team!"

"Even in the middle of the worst energy crisis ever."

"Yeah, screw the cartel!"

"You mean the *oil* cartel, and not our would-be partners in cannabis and crime." Lance fake slugged Eddie's shoulder, grabbed the plastic handle tied to a short rope, pulled up the garage door, and swung a leg over his motorcycle, disappearing down the street.

None of the criminals on Bobby Dunne's radar fascinated him more than the clandestine crew from Coronado. As he pulled a

TV dinner from the oven and peeled off the foil while trying not to burn his fingers, the phone rang from its perch on the wall. He licked the Salisbury steak sauce from his thumb and picked up the receiver. "Yeah, Dunne."

"You said to call twenty-four/seven."

"Denny. Let's hear it."

"Got a tip about some activity on the water. A schooner. "

"Coronado?"

"North County area."

"What else?" Dunne said. "Boating isn't a crime."

"Seems like more. Someone's got an NVD up there."

Dunne knew that while the offices were sparse, the government had spared no expense when it came to the latest surveillance equipment like night-vision devices. Well, almost the latest. Law enforcement was always three steps behind the criminals. It had been that way since the beginning of time. As usual, having money allowed you to purchase everything you needed to make more of it, perpetually widening the gap.

"Where, exactly?" Dunne asked.

"Carlsbad. Let's grab a few guys from the sheriff's office and go."

A teacher and some students . . . outsmarting the DEA! Dunne wished he could assign several guys to watch and follow. But the question endured: Where? There was a lot of beach in California—840 miles—and the Company from Coronado High School seemed prepared to use any part of it. There were another 296 miles along the Oregon coast and 157 miles in Washington. Initially, Dunne had dismissed these guys as small-timers. But now he wasn't so sure. He had to play this right to catch them in action.

Dunne grabbed his coat, and left the steaming TV dinner on the counter.

He and Grimaud drove up the coast, chatting about the evolution of drug smugglers and dealers, the general hazards of the job, and gun preferences. Both considered the old .38s "useless." Grimaud, who wore his blond hair long for undercover work, admired Dunne's revolver—a 1911 semiautomatic .45, polished sterling silver, with *Bobby Dunne* in gold inlay. It had been a gift from the Mexican Feds when Dunne returned to work in the United States, and he carried it "cocked and locked," with the hammer back and the safety on.

Once on the targeted beach, they hid behind a dune near a house they suspected might be a drop site and watched for the fishing boat, which soon motored into the area about a half mile offshore. Dunne and Grimaud could not believe their luck.

Then the waiting began.

Every once in a while the boat circled before reassuming the appearance of an apparently harmless, bobbing pixel of light.

Finally, Grimaud said, "They're not coming in. Let's get out there. We can use the Oceanside Harbor Police boat and intercept them."

Dunne stood to indicate his agreement.

He and Grimaud signaled two officers and bolted toward the harbor, calling ahead on the police radio to make sure the boat was ready for them. They made good time on the water.

Everyone thought the schooner might motor away, but as they approached the designated location, there it was, exactly as they'd left it! Spotlights. Loudspeakers. Guns drawn. Dunne announced their presence and requested permission to board. And in moments, the four law enforcement agents were standing on the deck with five guys, including one recent graduate of Coronado High School: Ed Otero.

They searched the hold. When Ed smiled and offered to show them around the entire vessel, Dunne and Grimaud knew they'd find nothing.

"Anything else we can do for you?" Eddie asked.

"Keep playing your games." Grimaud knew he should've kept his mouth shut, but he couldn't help himself. "You'll get overconfident and sloppy at some point. It's inevitable."

"Fishing?" Eddie said. "No, we're careful. Thanks."

Dunne and Grimaud departed and retraced their tracks to the beach, where they heard nothing but the wind, smelled remnants of seaweed, and saw little more than sand, sporadic patches of ice plant, and footprints leading to a beach house adjacent to their previous stakeout. There sat an unopened bottle of beer.

"They unloaded while we were heading out on the water," Dunne said, "and went right back out to meet us. Damn, they move fast."

"And we can't get a search warrant for the house?" Grimaud asked.

Dunne stated the obvious. "I can try. But a wild tip and footprints in the sand aren't enough evidence."

"How'd they know? Think they have an informant—from our side?"

Dunne crossed his arms and snorted in disgust at the thought.

At six feet tall and 185 pounds, Grimaud was larger than Dunne. But both possessed the scrappy aggressiveness of boxers—coiled and ready.

Grimaud reached out and slapped Dunne on the back. "Come on, Bobby. It was a good lead, but we came up short. Let's give them a chance to regroup, get ourselves on an airplane, do a little reconnaissance up the coast. Like I said, they'll get careless. And we'll be there."

When they parted ways after the drive back to Coronado, Dunne continued home, completely exhausted. Sitting on the edge of the bed, he shook his head and broke into a laugh.

This wasn't going to be nearly as simple as he'd thought.

On a sweltering day in August, every household with a television stopped to watch Richard Nixon resign, his face moist with perspiration but his voice remarkably steady. His family stood by his side until a helicopter transported him to Andrews Air Force Base, where he boarded *Air Force One* for one last flight to San Clemente, just up the coast from San Diego. A month later President Ford officially pardoned his former boss to help the American public focus on solving problems "at home and abroad": the Vietnam War, a lingering recession, and, of course, the war on drugs.

* * *

Sometimes Bobby Dunne thought he was the only person in the world fighting one of those wars. His attempts to trail Lance Weber proved difficult. The guy was everywhere and nowhere all at once. A jeep and boat trailer made Lance mobile across every surface. Lance came and went from the marina, other parts of the bay, or the ocean, taking care to do enough joy riding to make the agents fume over wasted time and move their limited resources elsewhere.

As their search grew more frantic, Grimaud and Dunne called each other with the slightest hints of leads.

"Weber's been spotted at the Glorietta Bay boat launch," Grimaud said.

"In Coronado? Radio the Coast Guard. I'll meet you."

When they heard from the Coast Guard that he was heading out of the bay near Point Loma, Dunne and Grimaud stationed themselves to watch with binoculars as Lance roared by, toward Imperial Beach, not too far off the coast, the bow of his Chris-Craft slapping the water, the stern leaving a rooster-tail wake. They scrambled to follow.

By now, several DEA agents had reached high alert.

"Don't lose him!" Dunne said into the portable black box. "Cut down on the radio chatter. Count on these guys hearing every word you say."

"Copy that."

Dunne and Grimaud ran to the deserted beach near the Sloughs, where Lance slowed his speed and turned the boat toward shore. Dunne pressed the binoculars to his eyes again and saw that another person had joined Weber. Looked like Ed Otero, the barrel-chested, athletic kid from the fishing boat.

"He's coming in," Grimaud said.

Just as Dunne held the radio to his mouth to give the order to rush the beach, Lance turned the boat 180 degrees, accelerating over the waves. Dunne could hear the boys laughing over the engine that sounded nothing like anything he'd ever heard—even on a speedboat. It was more like standing on the deck of an aircraft carrier catapulting a fighter jet from a runway the size of a matchstick. Lance Weber—nothing but a hippie with long sideburns and silly hats, from Dunne's perspective—understood engines.

Lance turned again. He was doing doughnuts in the ocean, a child with the best toy in the neighborhood, showing off for his friend, who also took a turn at the wheel and attempted to use the custom craft as a surfboard. They played for about fifteen minutes, then bolted up the coast.

"Follow them!" Dunne instructed into the radio, realizing the futility of the instructions even as he said them.

Grimaud stood and brushed the sand off his legs. "What a wiseass."

Dunne shook his head and sucked air in through clenched teeth. "Yup." He also knew the baiting meant that they'd find nothing. So he told his small team to abort.

They would have to wait for the next tip.

Chapter 13

1975

LOU HAD RENTED A PROPERTY IN NORTH COUNTY, an area that encompassed several beach towns thirty or forty-five minutes up Interstate 5 from Coronado. When he finally invited Lance and Eddie to see his new neighborhood, he treated them to dinner at the Albatross, an iconic Del Mar restaurant reminiscent of tiki lounges that somehow pulled off kitschy and elegant simultaneously. Its masculine, smoking-room interior reminded Eddie of the Chart House—except for the undulating ceiling that looked like a series of smooth waves depicted with pliable wood. Seeing it made him want to build something or even return to clay. Why not? He could buy a pottery wheel tomorrow if he felt like it! The realization that he could reach into his pocket and pull out enough for a sports car or a fishing boat or a house or prime rib or a plane ticket to anywhere in the world—*and* take care of his family—astonished him.

Lifeguarding came to an end when the "wholesale import business" started taking all his time. Even when he relaxed with some grilled fish and his distinct blend of Hawaiian Punch, or hung out with his new girlfriend, his mind churned over the next move, a possible connection, a better way to move product. Lou explained that rewards were tied to risk. You only won big when you dared to lose everything. Kind of like taking off on a twenty-five-footer at Pipeline in winter: It could be the epic story that outlived you. Or you might end up in a crumpled, bloody heap on the reef. In the language of economics, Lance and Eddie qualified as "risk lovers," according to Lou, who thankfully provided some balance.

During dinner Eddie noticed that Lou wore pressed slacks instead of jeans. A silk shirt with a flared collar and several buttons left open revealed his shaggy chest and a gold chain, even thicker than the previous iteration. His hair was slightly longer yet styled; the mustache, which came and went, was currently gone.

They sat down at a quiet table in the corner; within seconds a waiter displayed for approval a bottle of wine that matched the color of Lou's burgundy shirt. Lou nodded, and after a limited pour, swished and brought the rim of the glass to his nostrils, inhaling deeply. Another nod to the waiter elicited three full glasses.

"What if I want a beer?" Eddie asked.

"Expand your horizons first," Lou answered, raising his glass. *"Salud."*

Lance and Eddie responded in kind and tipped the delicate stems.

"Slow down!" Lou said. "This is a six-hundred-twenty-five-dollar bottle of wine."

Eddie coughed. "What? Why?" He set the glass down on the table just as another diner eased over from a dark corner of the restaurant to greet Lou and introduce himself to Eddie and Lance.

"I'm Victor," the man said, though Eddie knew that when the name rolled off his tongue so easily, like a bar line delivered to an eager woman, it was phony. "How's the wine?"

"Incredible," Lou answered. "The sommelier here always gets it right."

Victor, or whatever his name was, made a sweeping gesture toward the bar, directing his attention to Eddie and Lance. "Are you staying for the band tonight? They'll have dancing. The ladies love this place." Without waiting for them to answer, he turned back to Lou. "Speaking of temptation, remind me to tell you about a remarkable new hotel in Bali. I just got back, and I feel like a new person. You must go!"

They nodded and chatted about Indonesia until Victor offered a double handshake that included a grip on Lou's forearm, mumbled about having someone named Carlos get in touch with them, and excused himself.

"Feels like we're a long way from the beach," Eddie said as he watched Victor work the room.

"We are, my friend," Lou confirmed. "Victor has connections."

"That guy?" Eddie doubted that someone who worked so hard to appear refined could possibly steer them to a higher level of smuggling. "The guy with the shiny shirt is going to hook us up with the right cartel?"

"Yes." Lou held the rim of his wineglass under his nose again. It had become a habit before every sip.

"He seems like a prick."

"Of course. Those relegated to the middle always are. But we need to expand our network."

"I'm always up for buying another boat," Lance said.

"Let's get a real pirate ship!" Eddie gripped the wineglass as he might a thick rope and gulped again, watching Lou for a reaction. "A galleon's a good cargo ship."

"It's sluggish," Lance said. "And outdated. We need capacity and mobility, on the water and on land. You need to let us buy the DUKW. You know, the Duck."

"Oh yeah, I want to drive that thing." Eddie scanned the room for the hot girls Victor had promised.

"We need more efficiencies, more bodies on the beach to unload," Lou said. "We have opportunities to contract out our logistical skills. And I want to move things up here more often, away from Coronado. We need to watch our backs."

Lance shrugged. "People like secrets. We've gotten this far. Nobody's turning on us."

"People like to *share* secrets," Lou said. "And last time I looked, you've done time. I'm not cut out for that."

"What does that mean?" Eddie raised his voice. "We watch out for each other. We protect each other. No matter what."

"We're running a business, Eddie." Lou's cadence remained even. "And we need to do what we need to do."

"What *the hell* does that mean?" Eddie persisted. "This isn't just business. We're a team! I've got your back. And you got mine, right?"

"Of course, Eddie. You know that. But I'm talking about a truly professional operation. I'm talking about tons."

"You're serious?" Lance exhaled slowly.

"That could take all night to unload." Eddie drained the glass of wine and set it down with too much force, almost cracking the stem. "Guess we can get another one of those fancy bottles of wine, right?"

Lou ignored him. "I have someone in mind to help us get organized. A former student of mine who's become a good friend, and brought us an important connection. I trust him."

"Why do we need someone else?" Eddie and Lance asked at once. It was one thing to bring in a loader on the beach, but quite another to bring someone into a high-level position, which they could tell from Lou's tone was exactly what he intended.

"No offense, my friends, but you aren't the most meticulous planners. I need budgets and strategies, not approximations written on napkins."

"Who is it?"

"David Stratton. You met him at your birthday party at my house, and you've probably seen him on the beach a few times." Lou avoided their gaze. "Don't worry, I'll promote you both."

"You'll promote us?" Lance hissed. "We brought *you* in. We're partners, remember?"

"You can both promote me," Eddie said. "But I don't even know what that means. I'm not changing what I do, because nobody else can do it. Not even the musician guy."

The discomfort simmered. No check arrived. Lou gestured to the waiter, and he stage-whispered in Lou's ear, loudly enough for Lance and Eddie to hear, that Victor had picked up their dinner.

By this time the band was in full swing, playing a mix of Crosby, Stills, and Nash. Eddie never let disagreements stick with him for more than a few minutes. Now the bar scene was picking up, and he liked the fresh environment and unfamiliar faces, the change from the Chart House and Brigantine in Coronado, and the music—even though it was obvious that nobody should ever try to cover CSN's harmony. The stand-ins were currently butchering "Marrakesh Express."

"I want to stay," Eddie said to Lance.

"Listen, why don't you come see my new house? Kerrie's out tonight." Lou persisted: "Eddie, you're right. This is much more than business."

When Lou stood to depart, Eddie and Lance followed, almost automatically. The valet delivered a white Porsche, and Lou said, "Not bad for a twenty-year-old kid."

"Bought it from the Admiral." Eddie grinned. "It's fast."

"At least you didn't buy it new."

"All cash, all the time." A self-conscious pause ensued as Lance and Eddie stood by the open doors, each man waiting for someone else to break the tension lingering from dinner.

"You know you guys mean the world to me." Lou infused just enough passion to pull everyone back to the huddle for the next play. "Remember, we're the Coronado Company! And a team sticks together."

"The Coronado Company," Lance repeated. "Eddie?"

Eddie slapped the top of his car. "Lead the way, coach!"

And just like that, the family conflict evaporated.

Chapter 14

1975

JUST AS THE NEXT DELIVERY STARTED ROLLING UP the beach in repeated loads from the Zodiacs, Eddie showed up (okay, he admitted to himself, a little late) to find Dave running the show, carrying a clipboard and flashlight like he was leading a scientific expedition in the Arctic.

"Hey," Eddie said to him. "When's you're band playing again?"

"We're in the middle of an off-load that needs to take less than twenty minutes."

Eddie turned to three guys, which included six-foot-six-inch Lee Strimple, who had played basketball for Lou at Coronado High School in the 1960s, pulling a Zodiac into shallow waters. "Don't hold it like that!" Eddie shouted, running toward them. "You want to go ass-backwards? Turn the nose around and face the surf."

The guys shifted the position of the boat and started off-loading with Eddie's help.

As soon as Eddie's hands were free again, Dave approached him. "I have everything down to thirty-second intervals, and I don't appreciate you coming here and screwing it up. I'll give the instructions."

"What the . . . are you for real? You show up to our operation and think you're in charge? I've been doing this for, like, *four years*."

"I've been around. This isn't my first day."

Eddie shrugged. "I haven't seen you that much."

"Lou wanted me to fine-tune the logistics."

"Well, you don't know the water like I do."

"The hell I don't!" Dave shook his head and inhaled slowly. "Forget it. Can you make sure everything's loaded up in the vans?" He gestured toward the road. "That way."

"Cash only for the rentals?"

"I'm not an idiot."

"Just checking." Eddie grunted and marched up the beach, realizing that he would need to take a more active role in planning rather than always breezing into the crisis. He didn't know what possessed him to be so irritable. It wasn't his nature—especially with someone who was supposed to be on the same side. But he didn't like the way their core group felt fractured. Things just weren't the same.

There was plenty of money. So why did he care if Dave helped out and took a slice of the pie? But Eddie knew that wasn't the issue. It was like the family had adopted another kid, and all of them were vying for something money couldn't buy.

* * *

It took some time for Dave to account for every part of the load in a nondescript warehouse that he had turned into a temporary distribution center. He supervised the weighing and repackaging, and kept careful accounting records. After the warehouse had been cleared—they didn't want the shipment lingering for a minute longer than necessary—Lou hosted a party at his Solana Beach house.

When Eddie asked a sommelier to help him buy a gift for Lou, the wine expert happily chose a four-hundred-dollar bottle while chatting nonstop about the vineyard, the aging process, and a bunch of other details Eddie couldn't remember. As Eddie left his flip-flops near the front door, clutching the bottle, he tried to recall key points to make sure Lou understood the effort associated with the purchase.

Lou's house surprised Eddie. It looked professionally decorated with paintings, plants, artsy bookshelves, and furniture arranged in conversation areas with pillows that matched the color of the ocean in different weather patterns, as if lifted from a showroom.

Kerrie, her dark blond hair parted in the middle and flowing just past her shoulders in soft curls, greeted Eddie with a kiss on the cheek and offered to bring him a beer. She wore no makeup and possessed an easy smile and manner that made everyone feel comfortable. When Eddie had heard that Lou had met her in a restaurant, leaving her a huge tip (whatever . . . Eddie did that all the time, and the girls didn't move in a few weeks later), Eddie had been skeptical.

117

But Lou was paranoid enough about sharing his business with anyone that Eddie figured Kerrie might be cool after all. She seemed real. As usual, despite the many women in Eddie's life, he always wanted whoever was on Lou's arm. And Kerrie was no exception.

Eddie spotted Lou sitting at an antique writing desk in front of a window with a sprawling view of the ocean. In one hand he held papers, while the other stroked an enormous dog sitting beside him. Its tongue poked through dark lips framed in a white mask inside a larger ring of black fur. The dog looked alert and sturdy; it could've weighed more than one hundred pounds and taken down a few men with little effort. Instead, it was content to rest its head on Lou's leg, leaving black, white, and tan fur on a pair of designer jeans.

Eddie stopped short when he saw Lou smiling and nodding at the source of the papers: Dave. But he continued walking across the room, his bare feet sinking into the soft rug, past wooden—teak, maybe?—bookshelves full of Carlos Castaneda, Herman Hesse, and tomes about the teachings of Transcendental Meditation. It seemed odd that Lou would try to hold on to these philosophies, or even the books, for that matter, as he consumed his way to another planet.

"Hi," Eddie said, his voice brimming with its usual friendliness. "I brought you something."

"Eddie! Oh, I know this vineyard. Well done. Thank you."

Eddie beamed at Lou's appreciation, because all wine seemed the same to him.

"Don't want to interrupt, but, um, mind if we talk for a

minute? I need to run something by you." Eddie paused. "You know, old business."

Dave took the cue. "Sure. We've been talking for a while. You guys want anything?"

The clumsy exchange ended when Dave walked away, and Eddie reached out to pet the dog. "Who's this?"

"Prince."

"Looks like an Alaskan sled dog."

"He is. A Malamute. Pure bred."

"Nice house," Eddie said, still not satisfied with Lou's distance in the conversation. "Everything's so . . . I don't know. Perfect. A long way from our barbecues in Rosarito." He stared at the desk, now empty except for a green abalone shell gleaming with additional shades of blue, white, black, silver—too pretty to use for the loose change that had begun to accumulate inside.

"Well, I was trying to pass myself off as a decorator for a while. So I had to hire one to look the part!"

"You miss 'Nado?"

"Sure. I'll always miss Coronado. But there's more privacy here. It's good for us."

"I almost forgot!" Eddie pulled a folded postcard from the back pocket of his jeans, and handed it to Lou.

"What's this?" He stared at the picture of turquoise ocean skimming a white sand beach, deserted except for three wooden boats with oars—rowboats made to carry fish—and large rock formations rising a few hundred feet out of the water. Lou turned it over to read the note.

"From Bob Lahodny," Eddie said. "He's stayed in touch during his travels in the Pacific. Hawaii, Thailand. Everywhere."

"Bob! Really? What's he doing there?"

Eddie shrugged. "Sailing. Spiritual stuff. I got a few postcards with temples on them. He's into that now."

"Looks like he's having the time of his life."

"He went to college, too. Northern California."

"Good for him." Lou returned the postcard and looked at Eddie. "So, my friend, what's on your mind?"

Eddie glanced over his shoulder to find Kerrie tying back her blond hair and smiling at Dave, her slim frame disappearing under a loose, Mexican blouse. He reached over to pet Prince again. "I just, I'm . . . you know . . . Dave. I'm not sure everything's gonna click the way we want it to."

"It's already clicked. The last shipment was unparalleled. And we have David to thank for that.

"Yeah, I know. But I'm just thinking down the road."

"You and David are different. Polar opposites, in fact. But that's good. Everybody has a unique talent. I need you higher up, doing things nobody else can manage."

"You mean what everybody's afraid of doing."

"That's exactly what I mean! I don't need you measuring and crunching numbers. I need you at the bow of the ship, sword in hand! Do you understand what I'm saying? Let David do his thing. Nobody else can do what you do, okay? You were in this before I was, and I'll never forget that."

Eddie nodded. He couldn't believe he was having this

conversation and hoped he hadn't sounded needy or desperate. For what, he didn't know. But he felt better, and that seemed sufficient. He reached again for the dog, whose slightest movements distracted him.

"We're doing well," Lou continued. "I want to take us to another level. David is helping us become true professionals. Let's not screw it up, okay?"

"I won't."

"What I'm also trying to say is . . . maybe you and Lance can take it down a notch. We've talked about this. I don't like the DEA sniffing around. We need to be more cautious. More aware."

"We're just having fun. No point in making truckloads of money if you can't enjoy it, right?"

"There are different ways. What are you, twenty-one years old now? You don't need to burn it up all at once. And you don't always need to be a smart-ass."

Eddie sensed the shift in Lou's tone and nodded apologetically. "Sorry."

"I know. You're a good kid. Just a little exuberant sometimes."

"But that's okay, right?"

"It is, my friend. But you need to know when to turn it off. Now go get some food. Kerrie had the Albatross cater. Enjoy yourself."

Eddie stepped away from Lou and Prince, and took a beer from the kitchen. Someone turned up the stereo, and the sound of a guitar, harmonica, a hint of steel drums, and Jimmy Buffett singing about modern-day pirates resonated from speakers that occupied entire sections of Lou's living room. Eddie stared past the wooden deck overlooking the ocean; the pungent smell of the Company's product wafted through the open windows.

Lou rarely kept it around (well, he got a little lax at parties), but someone must have felt compelled to show off. Eddie spotted Lance, eyes glazed, a frozen grin on his face, a joint between his thumb and forefinger.

Others at the table were slicing lines of powder, bouncing up and down like toddlers forced to endure a formal sit-down dinner. The voice rose from the speakers:

I've done a bit of smuggling, I've run my share of grass

I made enough money to buy Miami, but I pissed it away so fast

Whatever desire Eddie felt to join the group on the deck faded when he noticed Lance's stupor. He wandered back toward the small crowd gathering in the living room. As he sat down on a sofa whose creamy pillows nearly swallowed him, he decided that he would buy a house here too. Or at least rent one. Then Lou wouldn't scold him about buying drinks for girls at the Chart House. And he and Lou could be neighbors.

Hell, Coronado was in his soul. They could move to China or Africa or hang with Neil Armstrong on the moon. It didn't matter. He and his friends would always be the Coronado Company.

Chapter 15

1975

LOU'S DISTRIBUTORS INFORMED HIM OF THE growing demand. Whatever Lou could import, they could sell. He could also see another business opportunity with the operation's flair for importing, off-loading, repackaging, and distribution—especially with Dave, who was becoming essential to Lou and the Company. The only way to obtain large quantities of reliable product was to connect with a major cartel in Mexico. His Cuban heritage always helped. But going to the next level was like moving from a game of flag football to the National Football League, with little more than a briefing in between.

It turned out that Dave knew a guy who knew a guy. He and Lou followed up with earlier connections and a few hazy introductions to "Rick" and "Carlos," only to find themselves victims of someone's strange sense of humor, or maybe psychosis.

Sometimes the mysterious suppliers told Dave and Lou to meet them at an appointed location, but never appeared. Lou tried not to let the shenanigans deter him though. He understood that many tiers of staff separated potential clients from the chief executive officer, otherwise known as the kingpin.

Finally, Lou received a call. This would be the day "for sure." So Lou and Dave scheduled their meeting time at Chuy's Restaurant in Barrio Logan on the San Diego side of the bridge. They would park, then drive to Mexico together in one car. But Lou showed up an hour late, intent on making a point with their Mexican hosts—without informing a now frantic Dave.

When they finally arrived at the Conquistador Hotel in Tijuana, the structure was surrounded by a ten-foot wall, resembling a fortress. Several bodyguards, perched on the barrier, carried submachine guns or twelve-gauge shotguns, along with pistols in their belts.

The scene increased Dave's agitation and made Lou question his late-arrival power tactic. He remembered the first time he had translated for Lance and Eddie in Rosarito, thrilled to make fifty dollars. Now they were staring at a potential deal worth $3 million. With the average price of a home still less than $40,000, one delivery could buy seventy-five houses! Well, maybe not quite as many if all possessed sweeping ocean views and backyard pools.

Two men with guns approached Lou and Dave, started speaking in Spanish, scolded them for arriving *tarde*, looked them up and down, searched them for weapons, and led them to the second floor of the motel, where the don and his entourage occupied the entire level. Empty bottles were strewn around the floor. Days-old food sat on paper plates that nobody had bothered to throw away. A stray mutt wandered about, looking for scraps.

They directed Lou and Dave into one of the motel rooms, where they found Roberto Beltran, the drug lord it had taken them so long to find, lying on the bed. Lou could hear Dave's breathing grow rapid as he pressed his back against the wall and eased toward the corner, his face drained of color.

Lou and the Coronado Company guys preferred handshakes and goodwill and reputation. But Lou could see that Beltran structured his business differently. Rumors circulated about former employees "jumping" from company airplanes—without parachutes.

The figure on the bed looked small, overfed, and slightly deranged. Lou understood that a subtle signal from this unremarkable man could have Lou staring down the barrel of a gun before he could blink. Despite a tingling on the back of his neck and the distinct fear that he might lose control of his bladder, Lou stayed calm and imagined that he was back in Cuba, a lithe, scrappy kid watching for bullies on the way to school. *Shoulders back*, he told himself. *Keep moving. Control your emotions.* Even so, Lou wished, for a just a moment, that an effortless translation for Eddie and Lance—plus a taco and a beer—would complete his duties for the day.

As usual, Lou offered a Cuban cigar, which Beltran sniffed approvingly. But there were no chairs in the room, and Lou recognized the peril of conducting business from a superior position. So in a bold move, he lowered himself to the bed, scrunched a pillow under his chest, and like a snake in slow motion, inched toward one of the world's most ruthless cartel leaders while commending Dave's operational expertise.

Soon Lou and Beltran were nodding and chuckling, a world apart, yet oddly in sync on a bed in a motel room in Tijuana. Lou's impeccable sense of timing and ability to understand people's desires helped him strike a lucrative deal with a man known for savage unpredictability. Gradually Lou eased off the bed, the way someone might exit after stumbling across a murmuring beehive. Lou nodded at Dave, who almost jumped at the signal to leave.

They refrained from speaking until they were back across the border, when Dave shouted, "What happened? Talk to me!"

"*Twelve* tons just happened."

"Holy shit," Dave muttered, immediately thinking about the required investment (a bigger boat, for starters), accounting, recording, weighing, shrink-wrapping, repackaging into commercial boxes, distributing, monitoring. "What did you tell him?"

"He has product. We have off-load and distribution expertise."

"Smooth." Dave could not hide his admiration.

Lou nodded. "Presentation is everything."

A few weeks later Eddie found himself with Lou and Dave and Lance driving on rough dirt roads in Sinaloa, looking toward Baja California across the Sea of Cortez, an idyllic body of water that divided the peninsula from the rest of Mexico. It stretched two hundred and fifty miles from San Felipe to the iconic stone arches of Cabo San Lucas. Shades of blue and green shimmered in the setting sun. Made famous in John Steinbeck's *Log from the Sea of Cortez*, the natural aquarium was also known as the Gulf of California—a place anyone could swim with a docile whale shark stretching forty feet, manta rays, fifteen-feet-long oarfish resembling fat snakes, and triggerfish you could barely lift. Great white sharks also populated the waters, Eddie knew.

Among armed guards and wandering chickens and other livestock, Dave, Eddie, and Lance started to organize the transfer. At one point, while Dave was busy studying his notes, he felt pressure against the back of his leg. He whirled around, only to find a pig trying to scratch the side of its belly against the rough denim of Dave's jeans.

When Eddie heard the size of the deal, he wasn't surprised that Lou, usually hiding in Solana Beach (or somewhere) away from all tangible involvement, came along to ensure that each piece moved fluidly.

Once everything was loaded, the Coronado Company owed a major drug cartel more than a million dollars. And they all knew that failing to pay wouldn't mean unreturned phone calls, as it did in their little enterprise. Eddie had watched *The Godfather* enough times to understand how a crime syndicate worked. They traded lives the way they moved product and money. Any punishment would mean the 1970s version of walking the plank.

Sinaloa, a cultivation center of marijuana and poppies and a globally recognized hub of contraband and narcotics trafficking, was accustomed to this type of activity. For the cartels, strong connections with politicians and investors who could front money and lobby for protection in smoke-filled rooms greased the skids, and ensured a safe operation. Therefore, Mexican police, called *Federales*, surrounded the area, poised with machine guns. Ever since frequenting Tijuana's Long Bar in high school, Eddie always carried cash to buy off a *Federale* who might stop him for speeding, or just pull him over for no reason beyond the sport of extorting a bribe from someone who seemed like a California rich kid. Among those who lived close to the border it was common knowledge and practice, because it never seemed to be an honest cop who stopped you.

The presence of *Federales* was pure necessity. But the scale surprised even Eddie, who didn't know if he should feel safer or more nervous that their new Sinaloa cartel buddies could hire this many law enforcement agents to protect a narcotics transaction.

Eddie managed the movement. A couple of key words in English, some badly pronounced Spanish phrases, and theatrical gestures did the trick. Dave spoke better Spanish and oversaw the *panga* boats shuttling to the fishing vessel. Lou networked.

The captain of the Company's fishing vessel called himself Charlie Tuna, and communicated via two-way radio. Eddie's doubts about Captain Tuna—a connection from an off-loader who was a former Coronado lifeguarding buddy of Eddie's—faded when he heard Captain Tuna reference the precise schedule of tides in Malibu, California, the destination of the cargo. Not every boat captain understood why the lunar phases and mean tide could make or break their business, and Eddie felt compelled to instruct them all.

As they ramped up for the big time, Eddie noticed a shift in Lance's behavior. But Eddie reminded himself that Lance could have 90 percent of his brain go up in smoke and still understand boats, motors, and the ocean as well as any of them. And he trusted that Lance had spotted mechanical talents in two new additions. Don Kidd, blond, bearded, and a few years ahead of Eddie at Coronado High School, and Allan "Fuzzy" Maguire would help them in Malibu. Fuzzy had grown up in Los Angeles and could dismantle and reassemble an engine faster than Eddie thought possible.

It occurred to Eddie that the operation could become too big. At some point it would be difficult to keep track of everyone and everything and make sure people didn't get hammered and blab at the Chart House about the latest gigs. But Eddie stopped thinking about that as soon as he remembered those problems had started with him.

Dave's obsessive preparation still annoyed Eddie and (obviously) thrilled Lou. What was Dave doing here anyway? He was a college graduate who would have made a successful lawyer or accountant. But they had made peace, for now, by avoiding each other. They understood that each did what the other could never accomplish.

The tricked-out fishing vessel, captained by a guy with a cutesy name and stacked high with precious bales, traveled around the tip of Baja and Cabo San Lucas, up twelve hundred miles of coastline to Malibu, far enough offshore to seem like just another fishing expedition.

In the land of palm trees and movie stars and a burgeoning market for their product, the Coronado Company principals and their growing team timed their arrival according to the tide and Captain Tuna's radio signal under a merciful layer of Southern California haze. A new moon gave them a spring tide—an ideal combination of no light and high water. But the coastal fog eradicated visibility, even for people who worked with aptitude in the dark. Nearby Los Angeles and all its sprawling energy consumption offered little help. In their efforts to move 160 miles north of their previous landing sites, they might have overlooked a few key details.

Dave had forced the team to rehearse ahead of time, which Eddie begrudgingly admitted was a decent idea. It seemed like yesterday that one hundred pounds amounted to a major shipment. Now Eddie watched thirty thousand pounds make its way from the fishing vessel to Zodiacs—each job helped them fine-tune transfers through the surf—to muscled arms on the beach to eighteen-foot-long Ryder trucks, hour after hour.

The Malibu off-load lasted for almost eight hours—a lifetime in this business. And they weren't in the deserted sloughs anymore. Cliff-side mansions sat in plain view of the activity; the only saving grace was that anyone who lived here also coveted privacy.

With darkness yielding to a hint of morning light, Dave and Eddie locked the back doors and started driving the lead truck to the rental property designated for processing. Dave had calculated capacity, but quietly hoped the small mountain would actually fit.

A few minutes later a pulsing red light stopped Dave's breathing. A cop car idled on the side of the road. In the shroud of the early morning fog, they couldn't see why. Impulsively Dave slipped the clipboard under the seat and watched Eddie's foot lift from the accelerator. A glance at the speedometer put them just under the limit. They squinted, trying to decipher the scene with shifting eyes. They remained silent for another few minutes, then burst out laughing. The policeman was giving someone a ticket while they drove past with thirty thousand pounds of weed. Had it not been wrapped tightly in plastic, the cop would have been able to smell the goods rolling by on the Pacific Coast Highway.

Lou had avoided the beach in Malibu but appeared at the warehouse with Dave, Eddie, and Lance, watching the process as the sun peeked through the window shades. Dave held a clipboard in his forearm, the specifics hidden against his T-shirt. Sure enough, Fuzzy and Don, the two new guys, had impressed everyone after repairing a problem with a Zodiac motor on the beach with nothing but a wrench, fingers, and a dim flashlight. It saved the crew hours.

Fuzzy, nicknamed for the thick hair that sprouted from every part of his body, turned to Dave. "When it's time for payment, you think maybe I could collect in, uh, product?"

"You want weed instead of cash?"

"Yeah. If possible."

"Not possible," said Dave, glancing at Lou for confirmation. "We have an accounting system. Trade would create problems in my books."

"Right on. When you guys are ready for the next barbecue, or whatever you call it, keep me in mind. I had a blast."

"Leave your business card on the way out!" Eddie laughed.

Lou reached for the clipboard, which Dave relinquished after a brief hesitation. Lou nodded and smiled. "Nice work, my friends. The distributors are ready, so we should have our money shortly. I plan to deliver payment to Beltran in person. A gesture of goodwill."

"You're going to carry a million dollars to Mexico and deliver it to a drug lord personally?" Eddie chuckled again. "I want to come."

"Let's get the money first."

"I'm guessing the cartels don't send invoices," Dave said. "So probably a good idea to get out in front of it."

Duh, Eddie thought. But he managed to keep the comment to himself. For once.

Chapter 16

1975–1976

BACK IN THE WAREHOUSE LOU, DAVE, AND EDDIE placed stacks of one-hundred-dollar bills in the counting machine and watched them whiz through with the ease of a fan circulating air. Dave stood by to catch jams. Most of the money they received arrived filthy and crinkled, so their guys went to banks, made small deposits to avoid tracking, then withdrew the cash in large bills. But not everything was as clean and organized as they would have liked, especially when managing thirty thousand one-hundred-dollar bills.

They wrapped the mad stacks, as Eddie liked to say, with adhesive strips and divided the $1 million into duffel bags for the trip. With their passports under assumed names and attire to match the destination, they drove to Tijuana and boarded a plane for La Paz.

While waiting in La Paz for the next flight to Sinaloa, Dave noticed everyone preparing to board with *Aduana*—Customs—stickers on their bags. Without these stickers, officials would search their bags and undoubtedly seize the contents buried under the shoes, clothes, and fishing gear. How had they missed this? Dave's pulse jumped. Unless he did the planning, everything was haphazard, reckless. He realized they were persisting on a modicum of skill and lots of dumb luck. When would it run out? The organization needed to tighten up. But right now they needed to avoid this mess. So Dave signaled Lou.

Lou understood immediately and started chatting with people in line, smiling, asking questions in Spanish and English, touching an older woman's arm, complimenting her pantsuit and hairstyle, thrilling her and irritating her husband and distracting everyone. Meanwhile, Dave and Eddie peeled stickers from other travelers' bags and moved them to their own. Nobody noticed.

When they arrived at the motel, Lou told them to consolidate the money in one bag; later, at the designated meeting place, Lou elevated the handover to a performance. Beltran smiled approvingly and nodded at his men to start counting.

"You come to me early, before I expect payment," Beltran said in Spanish. "This pleases me."

"We want to be good partners," Lou answered, his usual charm in full swing.

"Come on—you've had a long trip." Beltran put his arm around Lou. "Let's have dinner."

Dinner turned into a party. A group played traditional Mexican *banda* music on a collection of woodwind, percussion, and brass instruments. Eddie moved his shoulders and head in time with the music and watched a boy who couldn't have been more than twelve or thirteen, probably ushered into the band with his father and uncles, struggle to manage his tuba. Plates of *chilorios,* a regional specialty comprised of pulled pork and spices, appeared on the table alongside more familiar enchiladas heaped with beans and salsa. The cook came from the kitchen to greet Beltran and ask if he liked the new red sauce recipe. Seductive women with glistening lips and dark lashes decorating half-open eyes sat in the laps of cartel members. Pistols protruded from a few holsters, but for the most part, machine guns were the only visible weapons, staying with the men who guarded the exterior of the restaurant so the patrons could enjoy the festivities.

Beltran raised his shot glass of tequila; all four men threw back their drinks, gasped, and brought lime wedges to their lips in rapid succession.

"*Más!*" Eddie cried. "More, more!"

Beltran motioned to the waitress, who looked about fifteen years old, to bring them another round.

Lou started up in Spanish again: "We all want more, but we're not talking about the tequila, which is the best I've ever tasted, by the way." He paused. "What would you think about another shipment?"

Beltran ran his hands from the girl's ankle to her thigh, lifting her dress while she poured. If she felt uncomfortable, she hid it well, Dave noticed. She didn't spill a drop. Still, he thought

Beltran acted like a creep and wanted to make him stop. Beltran must have read Dave's mind, because right then he replaced the dress over the girl's leg and kissed her on the cheek; she forced a smile and filled the other glasses.

"To this beautiful girl!" Beltran hoisted his shot glass. "And her smooth legs and lovely black hair."

Lou, Eddie, and Dave followed Beltran's lead, feeling the room swirl as they tried to keep pace. Beltran said, "I want you to move some cocaine."

Lou shook his head. "No."

Beltran ignored Lou for the next few minutes.

Then, from across the table, Lou leaned toward the kingpin, his mouth inches from Beltran's ear, and raised his voice just enough: "We can handle twenty tons."

Dave overheard and started choking, his eyes wide. *More than the last shipment, which took us all night to unload? At maximum speed? Have you lost your mind?*

Eddie saw the look on Dave's face and kicked him under the table, which Dave did not appreciate. All of them floated in that treacherous space between tipsy and gregarious, drunk and aggressive. Beltran smiled and gave Lou a single nod while his gaze followed the waitress's ass around the bar.

Dave furrowed his brow. But even in his compromised state, he recognized that Eddie, immune to danger and sporting a higher tolerance for everything in the oddly congenial atmosphere, was keeping a cooler head. Still, Dave knew the coordination would fall on his shoulders, and it made his temples throb.

"You come back tomorrow morning, and we will play a game of *ulama*," Beltran announced with a grin.

Lou had heard of the ancient Aztec game. But tomorrow morning was already upon them, and they needed to leave.

"*La próxima vez.*" Next time, Lou promised. "We have to catch a flight. But thank you."

"Next time, we go to church at the cathedral. You must not miss this landmark!"

"How about the thermal baths?" Lou asked, playing off the drug cartel leader's apparent need to assume the role of tour guide.

"Of course. My family will arrange it. You will love our state."

"I look forward to meeting the rest of your family," Lou said.

Beltran laughed. "All you have to do is look around."

After the extended farewells, one of Beltran's drivers dropped Lou, Eddie, and Dave at their motel. As they stumbled to their rooms, Dave grabbed Lou's arm. "I need a few months to prepare."

Lou extracted his arm from Dave's grip and placed it around his shoulder. "You'll have time. We'll go north, to Half Moon Bay. One of my favorite places."

Dave shook his head. "The weather's erratic up there."

"David, don't worry."

"Right. Maybe next time you should join us on the beach to see what it takes before adding five tons you don't have to manage. That'll take us two nights to off-load."

Lou pulled his arm away and stared, silently.

"Come on," Eddie interjected. "It'll be fun. This'll make us the biggest pirates in the Wild West."

"We have two hours before we're out of here to catch a plane," Lou said. "Get some sleep."

"Okay, Dad." Eddie's attempts at levity did not help Dave, who disappeared into his motel room without a word. It occurred to Eddie, through a haze of sleeplessness, tequila, and too much spicy Mexican food, that he should've taken some pleasure in the apparent conflict between Dave and Lou. But he didn't. He liked it better when everyone got along.

Captain Charlie Tuna wasn't available, so he recommended Captain Dan, who agreed with the Company's plans to scrap Half Moon Bay and redirect to Malibu. As Dave had predicted, the return to familiar territory did not make it any easier. He designed routes, orchestrated elaborate backups, and communicated expectations. The volume unsettled everyone. The second Los Angeles operation, with a record-breaking twenty tons, lasted two nights—sixteen hours of all-out effort. When Eddie arrived (on time), he grumbled that he would have done it differently. But when they finished, he admitted that nobody could have executed more effectively than Dave.

In the warehouse Eddie stared at the bales wrapped in plastic, stacked several deep, fourteen long, and eight high to the rafters. A stray cat sniffed around on one, dwarfed by the volume. From a few yards away, the haul resembled the winter stash for a stable of Clydesdales. Waterproof plastic or not, the odor was unmistakable. Eddie grabbed a few bales and arranged a make-shift chair. "Hey, guys, look at my throne!" Then he climbed to the top and raised his arms. "It's like sitting on top of a double overhead wave!"

Everyone laughed.

"Don!" Eddie shouted. "You got a camera? Take a picture! We have to put this one in the record books."

Dave held up a hand. "No pictures!"

Don snapped a picture with an old Polaroid camera anyway. When the machine whirred and spit out the thick, square paper, Don flapped it for a few seconds to allow it to process, then peeled back the cover. They all crowded around to view months of work captured in a single image.

"Seeing it like this seems . . . different," Eddie said.

Dave nodded, momentarily forgetting his directive about photos. "I didn't know it was possible for it to look even bigger than it did marching up the beach for sixteen hours. But it does."

Chapter 17

1976

"PELÓN! WE GOT ONE!" DUNNE YELLED. "PROGRESS. Hot damn."

"Who?" Ralph Shaw wandered over from his desk, clutching a Styrofoam cup of coffee that he muttered was cold and thick enough to have been brewed the week before.

"Paul Acree. He was an early player, but fell out of favor along the way, probably because of his drug addiction. The guys bought him out and stopped calling him a while back, and now he's desperate."

"Stopped calling him?" Shaw ran his hand over his skull as if he were navigating a thick head of hair. "Is that code for something?"

"Actually, no. There's a strange sort of decency about them. If they want you out, they'll offer a payout and sort of disappear. This guy was busted for burglary, and he went into withdrawal while they held him. At one point he even started crying that one of the guys called him a 'total dickwad.' Said they hated him 'for no reason.'"

"Except that he is, apparently, a dickwad."

Dunne grinned. "And a weak link. Even gentleman smugglers don't take kindly to weakness."

"What do you want to do?"

"If he's willing to bring us more information, let's set him loose. There's no honor among thieves. So let's see if we can get closer to what we really want."

"Look who I found!" Eddie reached up and threw an arm around Bob Lahodny's neck, putting him in a mock headlock. "He came back to the States just to celebrate my twenty-second birthday."

About thirty people had gathered at Eddie's new rental house in Solana Beach, which offered panoramic views yet remained sparsely furnished enough to force most guests to stand. "And look. He wears *jewelry* now!" Eddie fingered the chunky gold of the Baht chain Bob wore around his neck and defended it as "traditional" and "authentic," immediately stopping himself when his gaze landed on Lou's gold chain. The evening had progressed enough to leave Eddie with an even more diminished capacity for self-editing. He hoped Lou's enthusiasm about seeing Bob again would allow the comment to slip by unnoticed.

"Great to see you again." Lou offered his former student a hug. "Where have you been?

"Everywhere," Bob said.

"You look different," Lou said.

"So do you!" Bob laughed. "These pants look like they cost five hundred dollars."

Lou looked down. "That's about right."

"And the collars sure got big," Bob laughed. "But you're right, I am different. Got an education, saw the world, did a little smuggling and a lot of meditating. Are you still going to Bula?"

Lou laughed. "Our sanctuary on First Street? No, we all live up here now, and spend less time in Coronado. Besides, I've found a different kind of spiritual awakening."

Bob nodded. "Fast cars, designer clothes, beautiful women?" His eye caught Kerrie in the living room. "Or maybe it's wo*man*—for now. She's amazing. Anyhow, Eddie told me what you guys have been up to lately."

Silence. Lou sipped the wine he'd brought to the party. "I thought you'd be climbing the rungs toward bank president somewhere by now," Lou said. "You have that potential, you know."

"Maybe I did in high school." Bob shrugged. "But I just can't sit behind a desk getting paid a salary. Actually, I could take the money. I just can't do the work! I'm looking for a good woman to take care of me."

"Lucky you're tall and handsome," Eddie said.

"Better yet, maybe you'll like my idea and invite me to be part of the team."

Lou guided them to a hallway, where Bob pulled from his jacket pocket something vaguely familiar to Lou and Eddie.

Thick, cylindrical, dark green, and wrapped in monofilament, it looked like a large, stubby cigar—only more exotic.

"What the hell is it?" Eddie grabbed it from Bob.

Lou reached over and brought it to his nose. "I know what this is. Hard to get, and very strong."

"Thai stick," Bob confirmed. "It comes from the flowering female end of a marijuana plant. To make it, the grass is wrapped around bamboo, or something else, and held together with fishing line. My buddy Luxana Phaksuwan—Lux—hooked me up in Thailand. Said I'd see my past and my future. They call it 'one hit shit,' because that's all you need. I'm telling you, it's metaphysical. A Buddhist experience. Businesswise, it's even more powerful."

A partygoer stumbled past them in the hall on his way to the bathroom, muttered happy birthday to Eddie, went into the bathroom without shutting the door, and vomited loudly.

Lou shook his head. "Elegant party, Eddie. Nice group."

Eddie shrugged. "Can't handle my punch! Let's go into the bedroom."

"Bob, tell me more about the business side."

"I did some research. The trade started in Orange County. Very low level though. Get this: You can buy a ton for fifty thousand, and sell it for over three million. It's more expensive than gold! I have a ketch that'll do the job, but I need help getting everything to shore."

Lou passed the wineglass under his nose. "We've developed a few things since you were last around."

"I can add value to your operation."

"Whoa, relax!" Eddie said. "This isn't a job interview."

"Sure it is," Bob said, and everyone laughed. "The truth is, I have college loans and expensive taste, and I'm broke. So tell me what I need to do."

Eddie said to Lou, "You know he won't steer us wrong. This could be good with the Moroccan hash we're thinking about."

"That one concerns me."

"Why?" Eddie asked. "Lance?"

"Lance has been . . ."

"A little *loco*." Eddie nodded.

"Inconsistent, I would say. He worries me. He talks way too much."

"Especially when he's stoned and drunk," Eddie added. "He's worse than me."

"He's become reckless. I'm sensing problems with Morocco. But I do like that it will force us to expand to the East Coast." Lou sipped. "Sounds like David just found an ideal location in Maine."

"Twenty-seven acres with a private bay," Eddie confirmed. "He chartered a plane for an aerial view to make sure it was exactly right. Also bought a new suit, a wig, and huge glasses for the meeting with the Realtor. He looked like a dweeb!"

Lou had been impressed with the scheme. He knew Dave had pushed for a lease with an option to purchase, offering $40,000 in earnest money, promising to buy above the market price. With that, the Company would pay a thousand per month. The buyer would make a profit and keep forty grand if the deal fell through. Everybody was happy. "It was a shrewd way to get us what we needed."

"It helps that Mainers—is that what they're called?—are sort of crusty and mind their own business."

"Plus," Lou pointed out, "that state has more coastline than California, technically speaking."

Bob chuckled at the information passing in front of him. "I didn't know you guys were already so international."

"Global." Eddie nodded. "Hands down."

"If we bring Bob's Thai stick across the Pacific, we'll need to keep moving the landings," Lou said. "David will scout Northern California. Eddie, are you ready to vet the sellers over there in Southeast Asia? We may want to do this one first."

"Hell, yeah! I'll go anywhere."

"Kenneth Eugene Cook Junior loves to travel, doesn't he?" Lou smiled, acknowledging one of Eddie's many aliases.

"Junior?" Bob said.

"Makes me sound like I'm part of a family business."

"Which you are!" Bob turned to Lou. "I'll need a couple of months to arrange it."

"Yeah, because we're going to Peru first!" Eddie pumped a fist.

Lou cocked his head. "Business?"

"No," Eddie said. "We're hiking Machu Picchu."

Though he already knew the answer, Bob turned back to Lou. "So is this a 'go'?"

Lou nodded.

"Enough work!" Eddie stepped toward a nearby closet. "Come on, you need to see what I bought." Eddie opened the door, reached toward a shelf, and pulled down a rifle.

"Jesus, Eddie." Lou stepped back. "What are you doing?"

"Celebrating my birthday!" Eddie carried the gun out to the living room and started fiddling with it. The Eagles sang "Take it Easy" on the record player. Two lifeguard friends yelled and jumped behind the couch. A woman yelled, "Oh, my *god*."

"I just wanted to show you the present I bought myself!" Eddie struggled to open the barrel.

"Don't point it as us!" one yelled. "Are you freakin' nuts?"

Eddie fiddled with the bolt action, mumbled something about a hunting trip and birthday cake, then returned the shotgun to its place in the closet. "Come on! What are you hiding from? It's my birthday. Have some more punch! Live a little." Then he slurred under his breath: "Pussies."

Chapter 18

1976

DAVE INTERRUPTED HIS PREPARATION WORK IN Maine to scout a location for Bob's delivery of Thai stick on the Lost Coast, about two hundred miles north of San Francisco.

The cross-country commute fatigued him, but he enjoyed exploring a place so untamed and difficult to reach that it seemed like a different world rather than another part of California. Then again, California felt like a thousand worlds, with no two pieces alike. He even found a few graceful bodysurfing waves that didn't close out and propelled him along the face for as long as he could hold himself there. A thick wet suit helped. By autumn the Gulf of Alaska started pushing larger swells down the coast. He knew it was high season for great whites, too, which sent an eerie sensation up his neck and made him want to scramble to shore. It was so different from Coronado. The water looked murkier, tasted less salty, and carried the scent of a seaweed bouquet.

They had to keep moving north to find more remote areas, to avoid detection. Lou's connections told him about rumblings from the DEA, whose agents were always watching but remained underfunded and hampered by limited jurisdiction. Dave was grateful for any legal limitations that prevented law enforcement teams from gaining ground on the Coronado Company. In his heart, Dave was more rule follower than rebel. So even as he began to master a lawless business, he implemented procedures and practices to make everything as predictable as possible. This eased his anxiety at crunch time. Fewer and smaller loads with higher value reduced the probability of getting caught, which made Thai grass so attractive. You didn't need to be a statistician to crunch those numbers. But the deliveries demanded months of preparation, including several contingencies for each meticulously organized detail, challenging even Dave's talents for strategic planning.

Treading water, shrouded by morning mist and an ocean shifting to a disconcerting shade of slate, Dave spotted a cliff in the distance. From this vantage point it could have been a thousand feet high. More realistically it was half that much. Even so, it was going to provide an ideal perch to watch for Bob's boat, the *Pai Nui*. They were expecting four thousand pounds—a significant (and merciful, Dave thought) reduction from off-loading twenty tons, with a better return on investment.

He rarely found time for recreation, so a few minutes in a hidden surf break made him feel giddy yet alone, allowing his mind to meander back to his nerd years in high school, when bodysurfing and reading *Popular Mechanics* made him happiest. These days he found himself fighting his cautious hesitation, trying to follow Fuzzy on off-road motorcycles along trails so remote that they needed to stash gas cans along the way. Then again, Fuzzy had built and raced motorcycles all his life, and knew no fear.

The nature of the business attracted wild personalities. So the addition of Bob Lahodny—lazy but pleasant and sensible (among drug smugglers, that is)—comforted Dave. He still remembered Bob as a popular athlete, class president, and good guy at Coronado High.

Eddie and Lance, especially lately, could be loose canons. But Dave knew that this line of work required people who did things nobody else could, or would, do. Who wanted to risk driving the seven-ton World War II Duck—a bath toy on steroids—around the streets of California? Eddie and Lance, of course.

Dave spotted a curl forming and positioned himself to catch it. After a few frantic strokes and hard kicks with his fins, he found himself gliding along the face, then in a small barrel, hearing the echo of his laughter against the cylinder of water. Seconds later he tumbled into shore in a roll of whipped-egg-white foam.

He didn't know how or why he had found himself in this position in his life. But he didn't know how to change it either. So there was nothing left to do, he told himself, except put his head down and get to work.

Eddie was deployed, once again, as the globe-trotting Kenneth Eugene Cook Jr. to the streets of Bangkok. Of course he made time for curry, the likes of which he'd never tasted, and Thai massages at parlors of varying repute, the likes of which he'd never experienced. Finally, the ketch loaded with Thai stick was on its way to California.

Then the ship disappeared.

Stuck in the doldrums? Had the captain run off with his green-gold cargo? Nobody knew. Then again, if it had been easy to ship illegal narcotics from Thailand to the west coast of the United States, the scarcity would have disappeared along with the high prices the product commanded.

Tensions escalated.

Weeks later Dave lost count of the number of days he had spent hunkered down on the cliff overlooking the ocean with binoculars and his radio, waiting for word from the *Pai Nui*. A disintegrating schedule added to his stress. He gazed down at the waves and wished he could find some time to bodysurf—despite the frigid water. It might calm him. Lou, nowhere to be seen, checked in regularly, his impatience growing. Lou not only stayed away from the action on the beach, but did so by ensconcing himself in a luxury suite about five hundred miles down the coast.

Dave understood the logic, but at this moment, with his cold fingers trying to steady the binoculars against his eyes, he couldn't suppress irritation that Lou might be sunbathing alongside Farrah Fawcett at the Beverly Hills Hotel pool. Or zipping across the desert in his Ferrari to Palm Springs for cocktails after a round of golf or a game of tennis. Or posing as James Benson to purchase another Mercedes. Or possibly flying to Paris on the Concorde to shop, adding to his international wardrobe of silk and linen. Or vacationing with Kerrie at his new condominium on Lake Tahoe. Nobody ever knew Lou's exact location. But Lou always seemed to know precisely where they were.

It felt like years had passed when Dave spotted the ketch puttering several miles offshore, waiting for the December darkness to thicken. Miles away, in a barn near Juan Creek, Eddie and Don Kidd eased the thirty-one-foot Duck out of its hiding place and headed toward the beach, where it would roll, miraculously, over the sand and right into the water to retrieve the goods.

It seemed that everything was back on track—except for the swell that defied weather and surf reports. Don advised Dave to postpone. But after all the uncertainty, Dave refused to wait one more night. Plus, Eddie saw no problem with it and chided Don for his caution. For once, Dave wanted to listen to Eddie. As the massive machine rose into the air and fell with a thud into the trough behind the wave, Eddie smiled. He'd been waiting for a long time to drive this baby. And whatever it lacked in maneuverability, it made up for in fantasy fulfillment.

Anchored but bobbing in the shifting conditions, the ketch required several rope throws from the Duck before unloading could begin; the two vessels bumped against each other in the chop, slowing the process. But the Duck could carry everything in one trip, eliminating further transfers and making this their most efficient effort yet. The math comforted Dave even more. If they could off-load twenty-five hundred pounds an hour, they could put this shipment away in just over ninety-five minutes.

Not bad for six and a half million dollars, Dave thought. *Not bad at all.*

Chapter 19

1977

SURE ENOUGH, MOROCCO WAS A FIASCO. THE original deal crumbled, forcing Lance and Eddie to fly to North Africa to assemble a new one. Then problems arose with the ship, the hired captain, and the product, which turned out to be a lower quality kief rather than hashish. Eddie and Lance found themselves in a whirlwind of travel to untangle the shipment to Maine.

During a lull, Lance drove from his house in San Diego's North County to an auto parts shop in the South Bay area to purchase a new camshaft. Updating motors in every piece of equipment he owned had evolved from hobby to compulsion. Clutching a hard-shell briefcase in his hand, Lance told the salesman what he wanted, and they discussed additional purchases. Then Lance placed the briefcase on the counter and opened it to reveal $20,000 in cash, bundled in tidy stacks. "So how much?"

"Um, eight hundred twenty-two and sixty-four cents."

"Right." Lance peeled off bills with a dramatic flair, enjoying the shocked expression on his consultant's face. "There's an extra three hundred for you. I appreciate someone who knows as much about rebuilding engines as me."

"Thanks. Yeah, I really can't take this."

"Why not? Man, you helped me out and didn't waste my time!" Lance exclaimed. Customers stared, then tried to look away. "Come on, it's my way of saying thank you."

The salesman glanced around and took the money. Lance snapped the briefcase closed, smiled, and strolled out to the car as if he'd just pulled a dollar from his pocket to pay for an ice cream.

Later that night, several beverages and bongs into his evening, Lance drove to a party in Coronado to catch up with his sometime girlfriend. Only he couldn't remember the address, and ended up going to three houses before finding the right place. He parked his car facing the wrong way on the street with one tire up on the curb, bumped the vehicle in front of his, muttered "oops," and backed into a motorcycle. He would offer to pay for the repairs, he told himself. But by the time he reached the front door, he had forgotten.

Inside the house, whoever it belonged to, felt like old times, especially when his buddy Paul Acree filled a plastic cup from the keg and handed it to him.

"Wow," Lance said. "Do I get any beer with this foam?"

Paul invited him to sit down outside. Lance tried to protest that he had not said hi to his girlfriend, but Paul whined that he hadn't seen Lance in forever and she could wait. Paul crinkled and rubbed his nose, sat down, stood up, then sat down again. Music, laughter, pungent smoke, and the distinct sound of snorting filled the air. The scene comforted Lance, who had been living in a fog for a while, adrift, uncommitted, overwhelmed yet somehow bored, feeling strangely external to his own business operation.

How's it going? What are you doing now? Morocco? No way. You started it all. You're the man! Think I can get in line for a taste of the Far East? You don't have any money I could borrow, do you? Swear I'll pay you back. A week, tops. So tell me more about your world travels and all the drugs, alcohol, and sex you can handle, man. I want to hear every detail, 'cause you know, I'm stuck here in 'Nado. Need to live vicariously through you. Paul's questions came in the relentless outpouring of a man deep into the sorry mix of drug addiction and desperation. But Lance didn't notice or care.

Even when Lance's girlfriend sat down beside him, he couldn't stop talking. Before he knew it, he had told Paul about the fake passports and names, the trip to Mexico that did not include him (but he didn't mention that part), their new lives and homes in North County, the Malibu caper, the dollar value of the Thai connections, and his wild trip to Morocco and Tenerife in the Canary Islands with Eddie when their seventy-foot vessel full of kief disappeared. There was no better person to deal with lost goods worth millions in North Africa, of all places, than Eddie. Nothing scared that guy! Lance described the bar scenes in Casablanca, emphasizing how every woman looked like Ingrid Bergman. He told stories of Tangier, a haven for spies during the Cold War because of its location at the western entrance to the Strait of Gibraltar.

A vision of the fire rings at North Beach skipped across Lance's memory, making him feel warm and relaxed—even though his brain felt like it was encased too tightly in Saran Wrap. Paul could be trusted. He'd been one of them, after all, and they had paid him a fair amount (was it $10,000? Lance couldn't remember) for a quiet exit. Not that it mattered, Lance told himself as he leaned over and kissed his girlfriend with so much tongue that she pulled away, frowned, and wiped her mouth with the back of one hand. Lance convinced himself that Paul was too far gone to recall a single detail anyway.

In the DEA offices in National City, Ralph Shaw approached Bobby Dunne studying a map he'd posted on a bulletin board. He was placing thumbtacks on the various beaches where their new informant had told them the Coronado Company had made drops. Shaw commented on how close to the office the guys had once operated.

"Yeah, I know," Dunne said. "You got any tacks in your desk?"

"No," Shaw said. "That's it for the year. Nothing left in the budget."

Dunne nodded. "We can't buy pushpins, the coffee machine is broken, and they expect us to go after guys importing mega-shipments with all the latest equipment."

Shaw shrugged. "Nobody said it was easy to be the good guys. Did you meet with the informant again?"

"Yep. Acree's an addict, so it's hard to wade through all the lies. But if any of it's real, we have a big one on our hands."

Now that Dunne was beginning to understand the size of the operation, finding the Achilles' heel was only a matter of time. Larger meant more vulnerability. As it was for the Greek hero of the Trojan War, the imperfection might be small and difficult to locate, but it could render the man (or, in this case, the operation) helpless. The frailty here was not a principal, but a minor player with connections to a major one. As usual, friendship and bravado trumped secrecy and discipline.

"If they keep moving . . . ," Shaw said.

"Yeah, it's a mess." Dunne shook his head. "If we can't catch them in action, we'll have to be more creative."

Shaw nodded. "Legal."

Dunne clicked the top of a pen and moved his eyes from the map to Shaw. "I might have enough to convince the US Attorney to pull together a grand jury. I'll get our pilots to keep flying us up and down the coast. If they're moving on such a large scale, how can we miss them?"

"Too bad you can't take a twin engine yourself."

"Better view when you're not in the cockpit. And last time I checked, they weren't offering me a plane!"

"Probably not in the budget."

"So let's focus on the informant. And the next shipment." He crossed his arms. "You know, I really think we can get that indictment."

Chapter 20

1977

ATTORNEY PHIL DEMASSA GREETED LOU AND DAVE, and followed them to their favorite leather chairs overlooking the northwest portion of Lake Tahoe. The afternoon sun glittered across the water. Since the state border split the lake in two, Chinquapin, a condominium resort with docks and tennis courts and luxuries that now felt like basic needs, sat on the California side.

The year before, Lou and Dave had purchased log-cabin-type condos there. They enjoyed skiing Tahoe in the winter; Truckee and Incline Village were just a few miles away. (Other favorites included Aspen, Salt Lake City, and Sun Valley.) But the new hangout also lured them back to Tahoe in warmer months.

Lou raised his glass to DeMassa, a criminal defense attorney who was highly valued among alleged offenders yet commanded little respect in San Diego legal circles for that very reason. Lou liked the word "alleged." In fact, he enjoyed semantics in general.

He loved everything about America—especially the innocent-until-proven-guilty edicts that forced the cops to leave him and his operation alone until they could prove that he had broken the law. In his mind, importing products people wanted to buy, as long as they weren't used to hurt others, was just another type of business. A commodity, pure and simple. And now, with Jimmy Carter as president, who knew what would happen? The DEA remained intact, but at the end of the day, it, too, was a political entity. Occasionally President Carter sparked controversy about the decriminalization of marijuana. Related street crime around the illegal nature of the drug trade was the problem, he argued. So while he wouldn't legalize drugs, he believed in changing the economic factors that yielded high profits and supported syndicates. Federal efforts to fight these unlawful elements were spread across too many organizations—some of which competed for information, busts, and credit.

Lou considered government bureaucracy his greatest friend. His new amigo, Phil DeMassa, agreed.

Unlike Lou, who exercised, shopped, and dressed like the wealthy man he had become, DeMassa looked . . . average. Lou couldn't describe him any other way. Dark slacks, white shirt: crisp, safe colors and styles. His shoulders hunched slightly, and his eyes occasionally darted under a shiny swath of skull that popped out from two tufts of hair over each ear. But his acclaimed legal prowess meant that Lou used Company profits to pay DeMassa's hefty retainer, just in case.

"Incredible wine." DeMassa sipped Lou's latest import, a rare vintage of Bordeaux.

"I'm always looking for the best—in everything." He smiled as his gaze turned toward Kerrie fiddling with bait and casting a line from the dock out front. "I love a woman who's not afraid to get her hands dirty."

"Will she catch anything?"

"Hell yes. And she'll cook up the trout for us tonight. You're staying, right? Dave's wife, Linda, is coming over too."

Dave nodded his confirmation. Though he wasn't a partner in the Coronado Company, Lou treated him like one. He was perceptive enough to observe everything Lou said and did, and make it his own: food, wine, cars, manners, when to speak or stay quiet. They perfected the art of becoming someone entirely different with a few props and mannerisms.

This way, he knew, he could climb in the Company, which had provided for his family yet also taken over his life. His hopes for touring the world in a famous rock band had disintegrated when he'd realized that making a living as a drummer—something he once felt sure he possessed enough talent to do—offered more challenges than rewards. Working hard was not the issue. But he hated laboring without the ability to pay his bills. His broken relationship with his father eliminated the military as an option. He wished he'd applied to graduate school after college and often daydreamed about a normal, law-abiding life. Despite the adrenaline rush and camaraderie, Dave knew that if given the chance to rewind, he would never put himself in this position again. Obviously people hired the likes of Phil DeMassa because they expected trouble, which filled Dave with even more apprehension.

"Of course," Phil said. "My wife isn't expecting me home until tomorrow."

"Great. Then you'll stay in one of our guest rooms and meet some of our investors tomorrow."

"Thanks, but I prefer not to stay in clients' homes. It's better that way."

"Suit yourself."

"Why do you need investors? You can barely count your money."

"We don't always have enough capital to pull in supply for the next gig. We're growing and constantly reinvesting."

"People in the business?"

"Some. Lawyers and finance guys too. One helps move our money through Hawaii to Thailand. Bruce knows a manager at the Bank of Hawaii who . . . facilitates. Why? You want to invest some of the three hundred grand I just gave you?"

"No, I'll hang on to this, thanks." Phil patted the briefcase and smiled. "To follow up on our earlier conversation, yes, the DEA is sniffing around. There's also talk of a grand jury. But don't worry. We can handle it—as long as you stay away from cocaine and heroin. Don't touch the hard stuff, okay? There's less commitment to convictions around pot, so do your part, and I'll take care of the rest."

"I'm counting on it. That's why I'm paying you so much!"

"I'm good at what I do, and kind of proud of the fact that the legal community in San Diego doesn't like me. Oh, and make sure to stay away from weapons, too. That will help if you ever get caught."

"Well, we don't use weapons, ever. We're businessmen.

Gentlemen. And we don't intend to get caught!" Lou paused. "Would you like to take a drive in my new car?"

"The Ferrari?"

"I have the Mercedes here. Convertible. Come on, it's a gorgeous afternoon. I ordered something for our get together tomorrow. Eddie and Bob are stopping by. We'll have a day on the lake."

When Lou, Dave, and Phil DeMassa arrived at the specialty store, Lou went right to the owner, who extended his hand. "Mr. Malone," the owner said to Lou. "Good to see you."

"Jake, how are you?"

"Wonderful. And Mr. Winter. Good to see you, too."

Dave extended his hand. "Please call me Darryl."

"We have the wine you ordered from France, and the special vodka as well, Mr. Malone."

Lou leaned in with a conspiratorial tone and said, "Listen, Jake. I'm buying a few thousand dollars' worth of booze here. You can call me Richard."

"Of course."

"But not Dick!"

The juvenile joke made everyone chuckle. "This is our friend, Phil. He's spending a couple of days with us."

They shook hands. "You've come at the perfect time of year." He turned back to Lou. "Mr. Malone, uh, Richard . . . I've taken the liberty of setting aside some fine cheeses and an exceptional caviar— beluga sturgeon from the Caspian Sea. It's very hard to get. And really, there is nothing better. May I include these in your order?"

"You are a fine salesman, Jake! Sure, and add some of those

crackers I bought here last time. The light, flaky ones? My wife loves those." When Lou turned into a different person, he went all the way.

Jake started to load an additional box and gestured for help from an employee to carry everything to the car. "How's the oil business?"

"Barrel prices are heading in the right direction. But it's nice that I'm not a slave to those fluctuations."

"Yes, of course. And your family is well? They are joining you for the festivities?"

"No, no, they're vacationing at our flat in Paris. So tough to get everyone together." Lou shook his head, fully absorbed in his one-man play. "You know how it is."

"I can only imagine. Well, here you are. John will carry these out to your trunk."

"Excellent. You'll put everything on my account?"

"Will do. Take care, Richard. Good to see you, Darryl. And nice to meet you, Phil."

When they climbed back into the car, DeMassa said to Dave, "Darryl Winter?"

Dave shrugged and Lou laughed. "Yeah, he was Darryl Summer in La Jolla! He can't keep track of the names."

"At least you have a sense of humor."

Dave smiled. "My favorite is Yancy Farquhar. But he's very uptight. Prep schools. Old money. Dysfunctional family. Kids who don't like him."

They laughed.

DeMassa said, "Sounds like eighty percent of my law school classmates."

The next morning Kerrie awoke early to prepare picnic baskets, gather towels and sunscreen, and load the wooden Chris-Craft Lou had named *Rich and Dirty*. It was a play on one of Lou's aliases and on Dave's sometime nickname, Dirty Dave, that arose from an eponymous music store Dave once frequented in San Diego's Gaslamp Quarter.

Everyone climbed aboard and alternated between water-skiing, sipping frozen margaritas Kerrie had blended in advance, and grazing on a constant supply of food. Kerrie loved Eddie and Bob, and made plates of nachos for them—piled high with chips, meat, salsa, cheese, chili peppers, and homemade guacamole that she drizzled with lukewarm water and lime juice so it never turned brown. The Eagles, Rod Stewart, and several renditions of Jimmy Buffett's "Margaritaville" emanated from the sound system. By the end of the day Eddie's voice was hoarse from singing along and shouting encouragement when people wiped out on skis—a guarantee when he drove. Dave's wife, Linda, and the other women who came and went knew they weren't hanging out with insurance salesmen, but they took their cues from Kerrie and didn't ask questions. And Lou, Dave, Bob, and Eddie never discussed business in front of them.

Back at the condo the men sat on the large deck, watching the water sparkle with each incremental movement of the sun tumbling in slow motion toward the west. Dave reported on the progress in Maine. Eddie countered that despite the bumpy but ultimately successful delivery of five tons of Moroccan kief (that nobody wanted to buy initially because of its poor quality), a different location would have been better. And they both looked at Lou, who rolled his eyes like a father stuck with two children he loved but would prefer to enjoy separately.

Lou pulled Eddie into the kitchen under the auspices of fetching more drinks and asked that he let Dave handle Maine, because everyone needed Eddie to prepare for the cash drop and organize in Thailand, where the supplier was allowing them to move the next shipment with a minimal deposit. It would be dangerous, Lou promised. So only Eddie could do it.

They regrouped on the deck and set a deadline for Eddie to pick up the down payment for their Thai suppliers. Lou touted the efficiency and ROI—return on investment—of the Thai stick, but he did not need to explain the benefits of less volume for more money. Thankfully they now allowed a few months of planning between each gig. Dave needed every minute to strategize. And as he sipped vodka, he pledged to design those plans far away from Eddie.

While the principals focused on the next shipment, Lance Weber grew more distant from the operation, but continued to party indiscriminately with Paul Acree. And Paul kept feeding everything he heard to the DEA to keep himself out of jail.

With their help, Bobby Dunne's quest to convene a grand jury gained momentum.

Chapter 21

1977

DRESSED IN SLACKS AND A SPORTS COAT AND armed with fake identification transforming him into Wayne Rothchild, Dave rented a car and drove to South Tahoe, Nevada, with a duffel bag full of approximately $100,000 in cash hidden in the trunk. Behind the front seat sat a briefcase loaded with $20,000 in small bills. He parked outside Harrah's, glanced in the rearview mirror, and inhaled slowly before adopting the strut of someone who spent his days gambling. With the collar and tie pinching his serene facade, he sat down at the craps table, played for what he hoped was long enough to justify the money he carried, then made his way to cash in his chips.

He cleared his throat and said, "The last few days have been pretty good. I wondered if you could change some of these into hundreds?" He opened the briefcase on the counter and smiled. "You know . . . for convenience."

Behind the bars the clerk raised her eyebrows at the pile of cash, moved her jaw over a piece of gum, scratched her scalp with a pencil, and muttered, "Yeah, sure, why not," before counting out a stack of one-hundred-dollar bills. Dave watched, felt his vision go blurry and lost count. Walking out of the casino, he forced himself to slow his gait. *It worked!* Back at the car he moved the hundreds to the duffel and refilled the briefcase with small bills. While the Coronado Company had mastered the all-cash society, finding a way to deal with the volume always posed a problem when banks remained outside the operation. Reduction was especially important for travel, and Dave's assignment was to make sure Eddie had exactly what he needed for his next gig. By now the deadline was fast approaching. Eddie was due in Tahoe the next day to pick up the money and fly to Thailand. Foreign suppliers, poor communication, and operations floating on credit always tightened the schedule. But as Dave knew, it was well worth the effort.

Careful not to overstay his welcome in any one location, Dave kept moving. Next up was Reno, where he repeated the routine before heading east to Sparks. By the time he arrived at the next casino, overconfidence and fatigue dulled his senses. And when he asked for $15,000 in large notes, someone was watching and listening.

A large man dressed in a suit stopped an appropriate distance away, then took a step closer and placed his face a few inches from Dave, who at six feet three, looked eye to eye with the burly physique and smelled whatever product was holding his slick hair in place. "What the hell are you doing?"

"Excuse me?" Dave struggled to steady his voice and put more space between them. "I'm . . . I'm—I'm just—"

"Never mind, dumbass; I know exactly what you're doing."

"Who are you?"

"I'm the pit boss here. And I know where you been. Cops called me. They picked up your buddy a few blocks away."

Dave's mouth fell open, and he quickly pursed his lips together to keep it from happening again. His "buddy" was Allen, another Company member who was mirroring Dave's progress nearby, albeit with less money. If the authorities had picked up Allen, they had his money, too.

Dave couldn't get enough air through his nose; the effort created a hissing noise, which seemed to drown out the hum and ding of the casino. A cloud of cigar smoke enveloped him.

With a disgusted twist of his mouth, the pit boss said, "Take your amateur operation somewhere else. I don't want trouble in my casino. Go on, get out."

Dave nodded, reminding himself that good manners always helped. "Thank you." As he turned, he used every ounce of willpower to avoid breaking into a jog.

When he approached his car, however, he thought he saw someone moving in his direction. Had the pit boss called the police? The briefcase in his hand was bad enough, but the money in the trunk? More difficult to explain.

He couldn't be sure, so he kept walking right past the rental car, across the street, and into a Denny's restaurant, where he sat down in front of a pie display as casually as a man with a screaming heart rate and rivulets of sweat cascading down his temples possibly could.

"What can I getcha?"

The waitress's voice startled him. He turned toward the counter and rubbed a hand over his face before requesting ice water and black coffee, which he knew was the last thing he needed.

"We got a special on pie. Half off." The waitress jerked her head toward the sagging crusts. "If you wanna know the truth, it's yesterday's. Can't really taste the difference though."

Dave followed her gesture, and noticed the mirror behind the baked goods provided a view of the parking lot. Now it looked as though two undercover cars were stationed in the parking lot, waiting.

"Sure," Dave croaked. "Apple?"

"Nah, we don't got apple, honey. That one's popular. Goes the same day. How 'bout blueberry? They're from a can, if you wanna know the truth. Still good though."

"That's fine, thank you." He paused. "Do you have a pay phone?"

"Over there. I'll warm up your pie in the oven. Almost makes it taste fresh."

Still clutching the briefcase, Dave paged Lou. With a hand cupped over the receiver, Dave explained the situation, probably in too much detail.

Lou said nothing. Finally, Dave asked, "What should I do?"

The tone in Lou's voice grew sharp. "Figure it out. But if Allen's money is gone, you need to come through. Don't leave without it." He didn't say good-bye.

Dave had memorized everyone's home phone and pager numbers, including Phil DeMassa's. Increasingly desperate, he thought some kind of legal loophole might reveal an escape he had not considered.

Dave called DeMassa, who sighed. "Think of something else."

Back at the counter, Dave ate two bites of pie, pushed it away, and sipped his coffee. He needed a brilliant idea—an hour ago. The only thing he knew was that eating stale desserts in Denny's would not solve the problem.

He paid the bill and left a big tip for the waitress, then slipped out and caught a cab back to his motel. He changed into jeans and a T-shirt and a baseball cap. The undercover cops were looking for a guy in a suit, so altering his look was a start. In the motel room Dave sat on the edge of the bed and turned the dial on the television, which spit gray-and-white static until he landed on the catchy show opening of a *Gilligan's Island* re-run.

The room smelled of cigarettes and beer and musty sex. He crinkled his nose, stepped away from the stained bedspread, and peeked through the curtains. He thought about paging Lou again but squashed that idea as soon as it arose. Was there another way to transfer the money to Eddie? Dave wondered what Eddie would do if he were here, in all his renegade fearlessness. For a moment he wished he were.

Wait, he thought. *That's it!*

Dave hurried to the manager's office and rented another

room, where he stashed the briefcase under the bed, then left the key for Eddie, under one of Eddie's assumed names, back at the manager's office. He returned to Denny's in a cab and called Eddie from the pay phone to tell him where he could find about $20,000 if Dave got arrested.

Dave spent the next couple of hours sipping lukewarm coffee and watching the undercover cops (now he was sure about this), and trying to muster the courage to retrieve the rest of the money. How could he get them to leave? A whir of sirens gave him an idea.

Outside the restaurant, with the baseball cap blocking the streetlights from above, he eased down Victorian Avenue to the Craig Motel, which shared an alley with the parking lot of the casino.

Dave clenched his jaw, then went crazy. He bounced on car bumpers, screaming and slurring half sentences about a rigged system that wasn't fair and how his girlfriend had left him because he'd lost all his money in the casino. It took about twenty seconds. Lights switched on; tattered curtains were pulled aside. A couple of doors opened, including one leading to the manager's office. In a place filled with nut jobs, he knew they would call it in.

He ran through the alley and waited for movement from the casino parking lot. It wasn't something they would usually respond to, but they were probably bored from waiting so long and determined they could take care of it, break up the monotony of the night, and return to their posts without losing a beat.

Dave had counted on that. And he took the opportunity to switch places with them.

When he saw his rental car in a now unwatched parking lot, he compelled himself to slow his gait. Sweat collected under the baseball cap; the T-shirt stuck to him like a soaked napkin adhering to a countertop.

Hands shaking, he dropped the keys to the ground and had to run his fingers over the dimly lit asphalt until he found them. He opened the door and turned the key in the ignition. It sputtered. *Please, please, please.* He swallowed and tried again. The engine fired. He backed out of the parking spot, careful not to hit anything or draw attention to himself. As soon as he navigated the exit and nearby freeway on-ramp, Dave stepped on the gas, accelerating right up to the speed limit toward California.

But it didn't take long for him to realize that there might be an all-points bulletin out for him. So he exited the freeway and parked on the street in front of the Peppermill Coffee Shop and Lounge, grabbed the duffel from the trunk, and—against his better judgment—returned in a cab to the motel to meet Eddie, who had altered his plans to pick up the money there rather than in Tahoe. While waiting, Dave's mind jumped ahead.

If the police were watching for him when he circled back for the abandoned rental car, there would be no evidence. He felt confident that he would hear from Allen soon enough as well. They wouldn't be able to hold him for long.

Eddie arrived with the French luggage that almost everyone in the Coronado Company carried because of the secret compartments large and firm enough to hold stacks of money. Dave, still rattled and fighting exhaustion, greeted him with a nod.

They worked briskly to avoid lingering at the motel. "I thought you had small bills for me!" Eddie said in his usual, high-octane voice. "This is way better. Nice work."

"It wouldn't have fit otherwise." Dave's voice was still hoarse from lack of sleep and, he guessed, terror.

Dave knew that Eddie wasn't flying out of Tijuana, which meant he would encounter more scrutiny. Together, they arranged the stacks so they would appear blurry on the X-ray machine, and replaced Eddie's clothes and maps in the center.

"Cool," Eddie said. "Thanks for the help."

"You ready for this?"

"I'll figure it out."

"You always do."

Eddie lifted his chin. "See ya."

At the airport Eddie waited in line to go through security, watching pilots and flight attendants breeze by with little more than a flash of their badges.

Eddie knew he was well suited to this work because even with a carry-on bag loaded with cash, he felt relaxed. His easy banter and disarming smile distracted everyone. People liked him immediately. The guy operating the X-ray machine seemed more eager to be part of the social scene than locked to his chair, so Eddie waved to him as he turned toward the gate, where he ran through the to-do list in his mind: certifications and clearances for cargo ships and ports, payments and payoffs to the right people, product quality and volume verification, tools to alter the identity of the vessel along the way, routes for tracking, arrival directions and instructions.

Eddie jumped from one place to another—wherever Lou told him to go—stamping his passport, drinking, meeting and falling for girls, getting the job done, loving every minute.

In fact, he was having too much fun to realize that he and his friends had become important enough to place them on every law enforcement hit list.

Chapter 22

1977

DAVE SAT AT A WOODEN TABLE IN THE TWO-STORY L-shaped cliff house he'd leased on twenty-seven acres in Cutler, Maine. Across Little Machias Bay was Dennison Point, an odd-looking puzzle piece of land where the Navy's VLF (very low frequency) radio towers popped up around the terrain stained brown and tan. Built in the sixties, they communicated with nuclear submarines in the Atlantic and Arctic regions.

The Coronado Company's East Coast landing site sat back from the edge of the cliff overlooking its own cove off Little Machias Bay and the Atlantic Ocean—so familiar and yet so remarkably different from the Pacific. It reminded Dave that each ocean fostered its own unique disposition. If you closed your eyes and listened to the way the water licked the beach—or rocks, in this case—felt the breeze deposit remnants of sticky salt water on your skin, inhaled the scents of sulfur, brine, and algae, and heard the distinct vocals of shorebirds and songbirds, you would know exactly where you were. Every glance at this ocean conjured images of a Winslow Homer painting, with some poor guy in a rowboat, completely overwhelmed.

Shrouded with a spruce-fir forest on either side, the house was too private to require curtains. Situated at the end of Little Machias Road, with a long, dirt driveway leading to the natural wood structure, it felt like a sanctuary. Intellectually, Dave knew that safety was relative, illusory. But it was nice not to look over his shoulder every five seconds, and he began to settle into something resembling normalcy while he fine-tuned the details of the upcoming shipment of Thai stick, now on the move across the ocean to Maine. The success of the last delivery inspired them to increase the amount to fourteen thousand pounds. Seven tons was a hell of a lot better than twenty. Yet it did not fit the category of "small." To complicate matters, the cliff leading to their bay was about twenty feet high; below, boulders littered the area. The isolation made it stunning, Dave thought. If you wanted to visit the nearest neighbor, you'd drive. And when you did run into local residents, they were open and friendly with a dry, understated wit. But they refrained from invading your privacy. If your ambitions revolved around social climbing, you'd be sorely disappointed. But for this business? Ideal.

Don Kidd had implemented a yarder—the same technology used in the logging industry to hoist heavy trees up a cliff. It operated like a huge winch. They mounted the system in the concrete inside the barnlike garage, then cut a hole about eighteen inches in diameter in the wall, where a cable from a spool emerged. Instead of pulling logs up and down the cliff, however, they'd move entire trucks—empty and then loaded—between the garage and the beach.

They equipped the vehicles with large, knobby tires to traverse dirt, sand, and rocks. They practiced between loads: You drove across a stretch of grass and shrubs to the edge of the cliff and stopped. Another guy attached the cable to the trailer hitch. As the truck began its controlled nosedive down the cliff, you stood on the firewall, legs pressing into the steering wheel, hands braced against the roof. At the base you navigated to the water's edge. Unlike Coronado, with tide swings of six or seven feet, these beaches had mean tides of around twenty-eight feet. Dave and his crew had tested every possibility and discovered they could manage them all.

Dave didn't limit the Company to one property in Maine. They also used a barn near Freedom as an equipment house, and a separate communications house. They worked fifteen-hour days to prepare for off-loading from the ship onto small, custom-made Kevlar barges about ten feet wide and twenty to thirty feet long. Souped-up Zodiacs would pull the loaded barges back to shore, where the team would then move the bales to trucks hoisted up the cliff like toys.

Another Coronado High School graduate named Al Sweeney, a 1972 classmate of Eddie's who had helped the Company generate a pile of fake IDs, joined the crew in the Skowhegan location. Dave considered himself a technology aficionado, but he knew to get out of the way when Al was testing wires and clarity and security with an antenna they'd installed. Hell, Dave thought, he could be accused of the same obsessive behavior with his sharpened pencils and meticulous record keeping of cash and product traveling the globe, the expenditures required to keep it all running—including a per diem analysis of principals "on assignment." No small matter in the financial crisis hammering the country as the federal government seemed to experiment with new monetary policies. Cash society or not, there was no escaping the mess of the stock market, frightening levels of inflation, and the recession that would surely follow. After all, the Company couldn't do business by itself.

Dave appreciated and detested Maine. It made him long for the easy beach landings of the past. Sometimes he awoke in the middle of the night, sweating and breathless, having dreamed about a shipment running into the rocks and sinking, millions of dollars slipping into the depths. The scene would occur just out of reach. In every nightmare Dave remained helpless, unable to stop the catastrophe or alter the outcome as rocks tore through the hull and people screamed, tumbling to their deaths. Somehow the scene jolted back to land, where men with masks and weapons chased him from his bed and his home. He ran until he collapsed, shaking as the barrel of a gun pressed into his forehead and strange voices demanded repayment for the ruined product or they would kill his wife and dog, even though he didn't own a dog!

Dreams were weird that way, adding layers to precarious

situations. It made him dread going to bed at night. Sometimes he considered smoking some of the inventory but thought better of it. Getting high made him want to eat and listen to music and remain inert for hours on end. Not the way to run a multi-million-dollar operation. So with the exception of a celebration (or some other worthy excuse), abstention was Dave's—and the Company's—policy.

However, something made him feel that he'd never escape Maine without paying a significant toll. You didn't come into this state, use it, and just leave. It was a rugged place and would take something from you, for sure.

After delivering the cash in Thailand without incident, Eddie supervised the loading onto the *Finback*, which had conveyed the kief a few months earlier. When the air turned crisp and set the leaves aflame, Eddie flew to Maine to help Dave (Lou was always changing his mind, moving people around, adjusting to the circumstances, but he made it clear to Eddie that Dave was in charge there). The water temperature dropped from chilly to a painful fifty-two degrees.

On the night of the arrival the team motored out to the ship, towing their Company-designed barges, stringing military-grade glow sticks on the water to light the way back. The guys wore wet suits—part of their uniform now—with neoprene booties and gloves. Don had created a radio system in a helmet equipped with a small antennae for furtive communication. Falling in deep water would be a bad idea, Don instructed them in his soft-spoken voice. But it was worth the risk to be able to hear and speak to one another while using both hands to drive and off-load.

From the beach Dave watched with the latest addition to his inventory of gear that a military operation or a modern pirate would envy: a night-vision scope that enabled him to see every phase of the operation. Once the shipment arrived in Freedom, they would begin the process of weighing, repackaging, and distributing. To everyone's delight, it went flawlessly.

When Eddie brought in a few investors who wanted to see for themselves how $20 million looked in a different shade of green, Dave was in such a good mood that he gave Eddie a friendly slap on the back and offered to give the investors a tour of the barn-turned-professional-equipment-house.

"Now the East Coast will have a taste!" Eddie bellowed. "Nobody can stop us!"

Dave wanted to remind Eddie he was still a surfer and swimmer from an upper-middle-class beach town. But Dave felt too grateful to spoil the celebratory mood. The accomplishment of a successful delivery filled him with a tingling euphoria—like falling in love, only better. He couldn't imagine anything else that would give him the same feeling.

Eddie, Dave and Linda, and Bob and his girlfriend arrived in limousines at the Waldorf Astoria in New York City, where Lou had been staying with Kerrie in a suite under the name William Rose. Eddie popped the cork on one magnum after another. Lou surprised

Eddie with two exotic performers who gave him lap dances and invited him to deposit money in their bejeweled panties.

This irritated Kerrie, who glowered in the corner during the entire, torturous fifteen-minute exhibition, muttering about misogyny persisting even in the progressive 1970s. She rejoined the festivities when Eddie came over, gave her a big hug, and apologized. They smoked cigars and sang along with Jackson Brown's "Running on Empty":

In sixty-nine I was twenty-one, and I called the road my own

I don't know when that road turned into the road I'm on

Lou and Eddie made drunken phone calls to order luxury cars that weren't available (or entirely legal, because of emissions) in the United States. When hotel security asked them to quiet down—politely, as Lou and Kerrie were practically residents at the time—they restrained themselves before bursting into song with Fleetwood Mac's "Don't Stop."

Soon the morning sun scattered harsh light on the merriment; Lou told Kerrie to schedule a restful day in the spa for herself and the other girls (minus the dancers, he assured her). Then he sat down with Eddie, Bob, and Dave in the suite's living room.

"I went to Boston to sample the last shipment, and the quality was not where it should've been," Lou said. "That will not happen again."

"Can this wait?" Bob slumped in his chair.

"Yes, but the next part can't. I just heard some interesting news."

Eddie leaned back on the couch, rubbing his mid-section from ribs to belly button. "Business? Now?" He then placed his head in his hands, between his legs. "I think I'm gonna barf."

Dave got up, grabbed the ice bucket, dumped the contents into the bar sink, and placed it at Eddie's feet.

"Thanks, man."

"Don't thank me," Dave said. "I just don't trust you to get to the bathroom."

"So," Lou said more forcefully. "Our man at the DEA, Mr. Dunne, has flown up and down the West Coast looking for us, taking the bait for every false tip we fed into the pipeline. I heard that we ruined his Thanksgiving last year."

"Oh," they muttered.

"Officer Denny Grimaud has been helping him. But I've heard from someone on the inside that Grimaud is getting promoted. And after years of tracking us, lobbying the US Attorney for a grand jury, and gathering evidence for an indictment, it looks like Dunne might request a transfer out of San Diego."

"Right on," Bob mumbled.

"Why?" Dave asked.

"Not sure. Overall frustration with the lack of support and resources to catch us. Personal crisis. Who knows? He might just feel done with the chase. Or maybe he's moving on to bigger smugglers."

"Who's bigger than us?" Bob asked.

Eddie sat upright. "Nobody!" Then he grabbed a pillow and curled up on the couch.

"It'll take a while for his replacement to get up to speed. I was hoping that would make the threat of an indictment go away, but DeMassa says that Dunne did enough substantial work for it to keep moving forward." Lou paused. "I'll check with my psychic about it."

Everyone let Lou's comment about his psychic hover for a few seconds until it evaporated.

"Dunne is an old-school, good-versus-evil cop," Dave said finally. "I have to admit that I kind of admire him. He believes in what he's doing."

"Can we go back to our rooms?" Bob asked.

Lou chuckled. "I'm an old man in my thirties, and you guys still can't keep up!"

They stumbled to the door, promising to meet at seven o'clock that night for drinks, dinner, and another round of celebrations and bonuses.

Chapter 23

1978

ON THE SLOPES OF ASPEN SNOWMASS IN COLORADO, Lou and his colleagues and their wives and girlfriends gathered at the top to decide whether to ski all the way down and finish the day, or grab the lift at the halfway point for one last run.

Eddie announced he would conduct an anonymous vote, then asked people to raise their hands if they wanted to go again.

Dave grumbled that it wasn't anonymous when people saw one another's votes.

"Boys . . . we're skiing!" Lou said. "We have wine and a hot tub and masseuses waiting for us. Stop bickering. I can't possibly do this without both of you." Lou turned his attention to the beeper chirping and flashing from the pocket of his multicolored jacket. He pushed a button and squinted to see the number.

"DeMassa," he said. "I'm heading down to the pay phone in

the lodge. I'll see you there." With that, he launched himself over the edge of a cliff at top speed. Everyone followed.

In a short conversation with DeMassa, Lou learned about the indictment in San Diego's district court, with the United States of America as the heavy-hitting plaintiff. It had taken a while, but Lou was named, as was Eddie, Bob, and their mercurial partner Lance. In all, the list included more than two dozen people. Apparently, Bobby Dunne's work had been solid enough for the DEA and US Attorney's office to make a formal accusation of serious crimes, shattering any last piece of anonymity clinging to the Coronado Company.

A meeting with the principals and their attorney was set at the Mark Hopkins in San Francisco. The late-afternoon sun cast an oblong reflection across the table toward Phil DeMassa, who had slipped in the back of the hotel and now sat surrounded by Lou, Eddie, Bob, Dave, and a couple of cans of beer.

"What do you think, Phil?" Lou asked.

"As your attorney," DeMassa said carefully, "I advise you to turn yourselves in."

Silence engulfed the room. Out on the street the trolley car screeched to a stop on the tracks. Nobody moved or spoke. All four erupted simultaneously: "What?" "Are you nuts?" "What kind of advice is that?" "You're supposed to protect us! We'll go to jail for the rest of our lives." "*Fuck you*, Phil!"

DeMassa smiled and waited for everyone to calm down. He was accustomed to criminals who could manage everything in their lives except the news that they might get caught or go to jail or come in contact with any spoke on the wheel of justice. Then again, these guys were not stereotypical criminals. They were former teachers, class presidents, athletes. They came from upper-middle-class families. They could have been professionals, wearing suits, and driving to work every morning. Instead, they were among the first major importers of marijuana in the United States. And while a few hoodlums had experimented with small airplanes, these guys had mastered moving huge amounts of product over water, because they possessed the unique skills to understand swells, tides, currents, and boats of every variety. Very few people could put all those pieces together.

"Come on, Phil," Lou said, slightly annoyed. "We're still waiting for some real advice."

"I'm waiting for you all to quiet down," DeMassa answered, unfazed. When they did, he said, "I cannot, as your attorney, advise you to do anything *except* turn yourselves over. However, I will make the following casual observation: We live in a very big country."

Everyone waited for the next part of the sentence. Eddie leaned forward. "Uh . . . so?"

"He's telling us to become fugitives, dumbass!" Dave stared at Eddie. "Are you tracking the conversation?"

"Yeah, I get it," Eddie said. "You're not *always* the smartest person in the room, you know."

DeMassa ignored them. "They're charging you with felonies." He raised a shoulder in a partial shrug and loosened his tie. "If they knew where you were, they probably would've arrested you already. But they also need more proof."

"That's why we keep moving," Dave said.

"Hearsay from disgruntled addicts isn't going to do it," DeMassa confirmed. "They need to catch you in action. But they're obviously talking to someone inside. That should concern you."

Bob leaned back in his chair and contorted his handsome features.

"Has anyone heard from Lance?"

"I'll give him a call, maybe get together with him," Eddie offered.

"That guy's a loose cannon," Dave said.

"Nah, he didn't turn on us." Eddie drained the beer and crushed the can in his hand. "Lance wouldn't do that."

"You don't know what people will do when they're desperate," Lou said.

"You mean like Dave here?" Eddie laughed.

Dave rubbed his temples. "Stop talking, Otero."

"Eddie, let me know as soon as you find out what's going on with Lance," Lou instructed. "Test the waters about buying him out. It's time. He's a liability."

"Hypothetically," DeMassa continued, "if someone who was innocent until proven guilty needed protection, he could send anything to me in the mail, and it could not be opened without a warrant. Attorney-client privilege is rather broad in scope. Hypothetically, one could even put property in the name of his lawyer, for safekeeping." He waited. "And another thought: If criminal charges are at stake, it's helpful if we can offer the Feds something. Or rather, someone."

An edgy silence descended on the group. "Not one of us," Lou stated.

"No, but more than twenty people are named. What about one of them?"

"With what information?" Dave asked.

"Strategic details that seem substantive but incriminate nobody," DeMassa answered.

Lou crossed his arms and exhaled loudly. "Other alternatives?"

"Do you want to stay out of jail?"

Lou laughed. "At all costs."

"They'll be charged with very little. It's your best option." After a long silence DeMassa closed his briefcase, then looked back at Lou.

"I assume this'll cost more than our initial three-hundred-thousand-dollar retainer," Lou said.

"That money has been spent—quite wisely, as a matter of fact. I'm sure you know by now that freedom is never free."

"Poignant," Dave grumbled. "You know what? I don't think I can do this anymore."

"David," Lou said. "We talked about this. Come on, now."

"I know, but . . . I just . . . it's not right. I can't live like this."

Lou walked over and placed a hand on Dave's shoulder. "Stay for a while after everyone leaves. It'll be okay—I promise." Then he looked up at DeMassa. "So what are we talking about? Twenty grand?"

"Fifty," DeMassa said flatly. "Until the next invoice."

"Damn, you'd better be good."

"You know I am."

When the door shut behind DeMassa, Eddie pulled a beer from the minibar, cracked it open, and set it in front of Dave, who could not suppress a smile. "So . . . ," Eddie said. "How about the South Pacific?"

SPECIAL AGENT JAMES CONKLIN—EVERYONE CALLED him Jim—settled into the desk chair in the DEA's National City office, a place that seemed to have evolved little beyond the hanging calendar Bobby Dunne had left on the wall. A mustache covered his upper lip and meandered down the side of his mouth, almost running into his chin, until a wry remark lifted the corners.

Bobby Dunne was pursuing other DEA work and awaiting transfer to another part of the country; his partner, Ralph Shaw, had been killed in an airplane crash while on a reconnaissance mission near Acapulco, Mexico, and Denny Grimaud, the Coronado cop who first tipped off the DEA, was now a sergeant and off the drug task force. They had left behind stacks of reports.

After weeks of reading whatever he could find—when he wasn't busy dousing the usual daily fires—Conklin decided to do some checking. Using assumed names (which nobody could prove, of course), Lou Villar and Eddie Otero had purchased Mercedes 450 SEL 6.9s, ultra-high-performance vehicles first shown at the Geneva Auto Show in 1974 and produced in limited numbers since then. "Favorite ride of celebrities and drug dealers," Conklin muttered to himself.

Who were these guys from Coronado High School? Lou Villar: a teacher and coach. Eddie Otero: a lifeguard, barely out of high school. Bob Lahodny: a former-class-president-turned-vagabond-sailing-enthusiast wandering the Pacific. They sounded so innocuous . . . like guys you'd want to grab a beer with . . . but not criminals!

Despite Conklin's enthusiasm, he knew his superiors weren't interested in the case dubbed Operation CorCo—simply because they were overwhelmed with the cocaine and heroin trafficking that created more harm. Dunne's transfer had left everything cold and idle, despite the indictment. It was like a yellow flag in a football game. Placing smugglers on notice helped the criminals more than the agents.

Conklin's college degree, tours in Vietnam as a marine, and years as a New Yorker gave him street credentials—and more. In fact, his father had been an FBI agent and always told him that the people you dismissed were often the ones who surprised you most. These Coronado guys were an eclectic bunch; put them all together, and they made one hell of an ingenious operation.

But not for long, he said to himself. *Not for long.*

* * *

At the Santa Barbara Polo & Racquet Club, Eddie held the reins in his left hand and tightened his grip on the mallet. One stirrup was a touch too long, and he made a mental note to check this detail when he swapped out his horse, which players did every three or four minutes. A strap pinched the skin under his chin. He'd never worn a helmet for anything in his life—okay, except for the hockey helmet with the built-in radio in Maine—and he didn't like it. But here it wasn't an option.

Eddie spotted his buddy Bob making a play down the field. The guy was a natural athlete—good at everything he did. He looked the part too, dressed in the tight pants and high boots that made Eddie feel ridiculous, like Bob might have been royalty on holiday, picking up a game because his mood and the weather aligned.

The solid ball flew in Eddie's direction. He stood off the saddle; with the slightest tap from his heels and a brush of rein against the neck, Eddie's pony, which had what club experts called a "light mouth," ran full tilt toward the action, ears twitching. Eddie caught a glimpse of a young woman in a floppy hat, sipping champagne and navigating the lawn in her high heels. He whooped loudly. People stared. A teammate yelled at him to focus on the game. Eddie laughed. The formality of this place blew his mind!

In fact, only white was allowed on the tennis courts. Who cared what color you wore? They did, apparently, because when Eddie walked onto the tennis court in a green T-shirt one day, they kicked him off. Instead, he watched a tennis ball bounce between Lou and Bob, both dressed as though money had coursed through their families' veins for generations.

Bob had become acquainted with Santa Barbara through his new-age friends who favored ancient yoga and experimental drugs. He bought a Spanish-style villa with a tennis court, pool, and stables in Montecito, which was Santa Barbara, only more so: affluent, discreet, and spacious, with sweeping ocean views from a slight elevation. One long weekend at Bob's estate gave Eddie enough of Montecito to know he wanted to live there too. The casual beach town reminded him of Coronado, with a slight desert feel to it. He liked gathering for cocktails at the Biltmore Hotel on the cliff overlooking the beach and feeling part of the easy wealth seeping from every pricey property, high-end car, chic boutique, and stunning blonde.

So he bought a house nearby. Lou did the same, and also purchased a property in Hilton Head, South Carolina. Soon Eddie and Bob had joined the Santa Barbara Polo Club, and before long, owned a few dozen polo ponies between them. Why not? It was the thing to do. They also donated to charities, drank afternoon martinis with businessmen and politicians, accepted every invitation they received, and hosted extravagant parties.

One of the most memorable celebrated Eddie's twenty-fourth birthday and a profitable delivery of Thai stick to Bear Harbor in Northern California. He issued verbal invitations over a series of days to acquaintances from the polo club, the hottest waitresses from his favorite restaurants, and all his friends in the Coronado Company—including Lance Weber. If the guy was messing up, Eddie wanted to help him get back on track.

Holding a glass of wine, Phil DeMassa scanned the crowd and the sprawl of catered food, complete with live cooking stations, before pulling Lou and Eddie toward him. Almost yelling over the Rolling Stones, DeMassa issued a warning: "Great party, Eddie. But it's a little over the top, don't you think? I mean, who are these people?"

"My friends!"

"Can you turn down the music? The police will show up at ten o'clock. It's a quiet neighborhood."

"I invited all the neighbors! Nobody cares! Don't be such a downer on my birthday, Phil."

"Do I need to remind you that you are fugitives—in *hiding*?" DeMassa paused, looking to Lou for support. "It's derived from the Latin *fugitivus*, related to the word 'flee.' Which, I might add, you do not appear to be doing."

Lou shrugged. "We're hiding in plain sight. It's the best way. When people see that you have money and don't reveal anything about yourself, they become fascinated. They want to be near you, but they leave you alone. Besides, what's the sense in working so hard if we can't enjoy it a little, right? Listen, Phil, take the night off. Enjoy a taste of the delicious food and fabulous women. I'll make sure Eddie and Bob rein it in a little. Starting tomorrow. Okay?"

"Rein it in? Your humor disappoints me, Lou." DeMassa chuckled and sipped his wine. "I am having fun. I'm just watching out for you." He glanced out to the back patio, where Lance had gathered a group; clouds carried a caustic scent that wafted into the house and made DeMassa's eyes water.

Lou followed his gaze. "Eddie, what's Lance doing here?"

"You told me to follow up. Besides, he kept calling. I felt bad. He brought us in, remember?"

DeMassa interjected, "I'll remind you that there's little room for sentiment when it comes to staying out of jail. You're ignoring my warnings about Paul Acree, who might be talking to the DEA."

"Paul's a dick," Eddie said. "And he doesn't know anything."

"What matters is *who* he knows," DeMassa said. "Any information is currency."

Lou nodded. "I'll talk to Lance."

"I'll come with you," Eddie said. "I just . . . He's family, you know? Can we give him another chance? I mean, he's employee number one, right?"

"Listen, Eddie. People change. This isn't right for him anymore. We're doing him a favor by allowing him to find something that suits him better. Think of it like that."

Eddie and Lou walked out to the patio and gestured for Lance to stop prepping the bowl and join them off to the side.

"What's up?" Lance's words bounced through a series of shallow breaths, as though he'd been running circles around the yard. His eyes looked bloodshot and unfocused. "I was in the middle of an epic story."

"Just checking on you," Lou said.

"I'm good, I'm good! Why?"

"You had any contact with Paul Acree lately?" Lou asked.

"What? Uh, I don't know. Probably not." A nervous laugh escaped him, and Lance pushed hair out of his face. "Some nice product you guys brought in, I'll tell you that."

Lou lowered his voice. "Lance, the product is to sell to our distributors, not smoke."

"Right, okay. I've seen you smoking and snorting, and now there's all these rules!" He held his hands up in mock defense. "My mistake!"

Lou took a few more steps away from the group. Eddie followed. "Lance." Lou waited for Lance to move closer. "I'm not perfect. But I'm always in charge of what I'm doing. In your case, the substances control you. And that can't happen."

"What's going on?" Lance said. "You guys are acting weird."

"*We're* acting weird?" Lou said. "I'm afraid the problem lies with you, my friend. You've become too unreliable. And you don't know when to stop talking."

"What's happening?" Lance's voice jumped an octave. "I feel like something's happening."

"I'll call you tomorrow," Lou said firmly. "We'll talk then."

"No." Lance crossed his arms. "Now."

"This isn't the place, Lance."

"Wait." He fingered the greasy hair brushing his shoulders and paced in a circle. "Are you guys kicking me out of the business *I* started? That's, like, not possible! Did you forget this was *my* idea? Is that what's happening here?"

"Lance, hey." Eddie slapped Lance's shoulder harder than he meant to. "I invited you to my birthday party!"

Lance jerked away. "You can't just leave me. It's like telling me to get out of my own house, like cutting me out of the family. I'm named in the indictment, too." He stumbled over the word "indictment," and paused. "Lou? Remember what you were doing when I brought you in? Man, you were painting a goddamned *house*? Where would you be if I hadn't rescued you from your pathetic life?"

"Lance, I am grateful." The words chafed at Lou, but he censored the urge to do anything other than lean in as though he were speaking with a troubled student. "And you're right, we're a family. So why don't I give you a call tomorrow, and we'll sort this out more quietly?"

"You can't do this! But you know what? It doesn't matter, because I'm done anyways. I got other things going on. Deals brewing." Lance marched back to his once-captive groupies, grabbed the remaining product from the picnic table, and started into the house.

"Could you do us a favor and leave from the side gate?" Lou said.

"Sorry!" Eddie called out in an earnest tone.

Back inside, Lou and Eddie reconvened with Phil DeMassa, even as the party raged around them. Two women danced against each other, back to front, to the Bee Gees singing "Stayin' Alive." Eddie felt sorry for Lance, but there wasn't much you could do for someone hell-bent on his own destruction.

When they told DeMassa what had transpired outside, the attorney became impassive. "Do not have any more contact with him. I'll reach out with a settlement so you can purchase his portion of the business."

"How do we figure that?" Eddie asked.

"Pretty hard to come up with a valuation," DeMassa acknowledged. "How does a hundred and fifty thousand sound?"

"He hasn't been engaged for a while," Lou confirmed. "Still. Maybe two fifty? For his role as a founding partner."

"We spent more than that on cars last year," Eddie said. "How about four? Might make him feel better."

"I've never seen clients worry so much about people's feelings."

"You don't understand," Eddie said. "It's not just a business. We're . . ."

"Connected," Lou finished.

"Yeah." Eddie nodded.

"Time to disconnect," DeMassa said. "There's an indictment, in case you've forgotten."

A few days later Lance met Phil DeMassa in a parking lot in Orange County; they exchanged niceties, but little more. DeMassa considered Lance an encumbrance to the Company, whose members could not pay his astronomical fees if they went to jail. So DeMassa was protecting his own interests as much as theirs.

In the harsh light of day Lance looked frail, wan, hungover. "Is this mine?" He gestured to the briefcase DeMassa had set down between them.

"I believe so." DeMassa turned to leave. "Take care, Lance. Watch yourself."

When DeMassa drove away, Lance slipped into his car, opened the briefcase, and counted. He did it again, then slammed the lid, yelling a streak of obscenities and swatting the steering wheel. He tore out of the parking lot to the nearest pay phone to page Lou.

"You push me out and then you cheat me? What the *fuck*?"

"What do you mean?" Lou said. "Nobody's cheating anybody. That's not how we do business."

"We agreed on four hundred thousand. Phil brokered the deal. He *told* me four. And you know how much I got?"

"No." Lou sat perfectly still the way Bula had taught him during their meditations.

"A hundred and eighty! That's . . . that's . . . less than *half*!"

"Didn't Phil tell you about his transaction fee?" Lou's voice remained calm, smooth. "He's expensive. But worth it."

"You should just kill me. Like a real cartel, instead of this . . . I don't know, lame gentlemen's club or whatever you're running since you took it from me."

"You don't mean that, Lance. Do you?"

Lance tried to swallow the fireball forming in his throat.

"We prefer to operate a more civilized business," Lou continued. "And I think that's what you always intended. I'm sorry you're upset, but this is where we are."

"This is where we are? Do you hear yourself? You're a prick, Lou. You know that? My ass is on the line too! More, since I've been to prison. You haven't. You don't know what it's like." Memories of Lompoc flooded his consciousness. His voice cracked. "And if you don't stand by your family, they won't stand by you, either. This thing . . . everything you have, it can't last forever. It'll all go to hell."

Lou wondered for a split second if this were true, but then chided himself for listening to a guy writhing in his own hurt feelings and inadequacy. Who wanted to be uninvited from the cool crowd? Getting left out felt terrible, he knew (or at least he guessed; it had been a very long time since he'd felt excluded from anything he wanted, and he had no intention of reliving any of it). Still, the whole exchange left him uneasy. "Lance, take care. I know you'll do the right thing."

When Lou hung up, Lance stared at the receiver before looking one way down the street, then the other. People walking, cars driving by, signs, traffic lights—everything looked hazy. Where would he go now? What would he do? He hadn't worked a real job since . . . ever. And here he was, in his midthirties. An old man! The money had made it so easy to consume everything in his path; at this point he couldn't control his spending, his squandering. He would run out. Soon. He wondered if he could start a business selling or repairing boats. Something he liked. Make an honest living. Maybe even marry a nice girl and settle down in Coronado.

His bottom lip quivered, and he tucked it between his teeth to make it stop. Now that he was off the phone, done acting like the tough guy he knew he wasn't, he couldn't stop the tears forcing their way out. He wiped his eyes before the impotence could escape to his cheek and walked back to the car, clutching the briefcase that felt like his last hope. As usual, it amounted to way less than he had anticipated. And that, he decided, completely sucked.

Chapter 25

1978

GIVEN THEIR STATUS AS FUGITIVES, MEMBERS OF THE Coronado Company continued to diversify their business with new suppliers and product from different parts of the world, careful to avoid patterns that might be tracked. This created constant challenges for everyone, but kept things especially interesting for Eddie.

On this occasion he packed a suitcase and sifted through his stack of passports, pondering which name to use for the next mission. A contractor hired to carry five tons of Pakistani hashish to Maine had disappeared, as people in this business tended to do—intentionally or not. He could have been told to take a swim in some faraway ocean, or just descended into a blur of alcohol and drugs. Luckily, the product hadn't left with him, so Eddie just needed to arrange for a new ship and captain and move the cargo.

Time and again Eddie had proven his ability to manage the operation in foreign ports, scout growers, screen product, find reliable people to bribe authorities, secure a boat, assemble a crew. In Thailand he had even made time to see architecture with pointy gold spires, and rub every Buddha belly he saw, which Bob promised would bring him good luck.

This time he landed about a thousand miles south, in Singapore. Eddie thrived in new environments, and this was no different. School may not have been his strength, but his instincts, street smarts, utter fearlessness, and ability to communicate in the universal language of American dollars served him well.

In Singapore he settled into an airport hotel, transferring to accommodations near the marina the next day. One key contact led him to another, but Eddie took care to walk the pristine, modern streets wearing a pair of glasses and an ironed shirt, posing as a scientist looking for a research vessel to study coral reefs. He settled on the *Tusker*: 130 feet from bow to stern, with a nifty, hidden cargo hold and an owner willing to take a briefcase full of cash in return for some flexibility.

Eddie directed every step of the *Tusker's* travels through the Indian Ocean and Arabian Sea to Bombay, India, where he made sure the Pakistani hashish crossed the border and found its way aboard with nautical charts, Mylar films, grease pencils, provisions, and satellite radios to communicate with Dave and Al Sweeney in Maine. Going through the Suez Canal was out of the question for security reasons, so they plotted the much longer route around South Africa. Soon the *Tusker* was on its way to the North Atlantic.

Meanwhile, Eddie flew back to Maine to await its arrival. But as soon as they thought the delivery was back on track, the ship faded away. It was a long journey, everyone knew. Hearing nothing but static, however—especially after plan A had fallen apart—put the crew on edge.

Periods of intense activity followed by long stretches of waiting tested Dave. It wasn't like he could relax during the interlude. Right now everyone grated on his nerves. He wished Al would shut up about the radios. Done with their prep work, Fuzzy and Don squabbled constantly. At night Dave lay awake as though he'd gulped three espressos right before bed. The more exhausted he became, the less he slept.

Dave struggled to go about his daily routine as quietly as possible—even when he wanted to holler in frustration. Despite the Company's caution with suppliers and movement on the ocean, the crew had grown too comfortable with Maine and careless about the appearance of activity in and out of the Machias cliff house. The longer they lived there, the more concerned he became. To limit his exposure, Dave sometimes hid on the floor of the car while another employee posing as a property manager drove him to and from the house.

On this particular afternoon Dave finished checking the status of the off-load area (again) with a new hire named Andy, and hopped in the driver's seat. He didn't have the energy to crouch on the floor. As soon as they pulled onto the road, Dave saw a man parked in a brown sedan do a double take before flipping a tight U-turn to follow them. While the other Company guys bought fancy cars, Dave preferred a Chevy Blazer. Of course he let Fuzzy install a few upgrades so it could accelerate like a Ferrari. For the most part, he could move around under the radar.

Dave stared into the rearview mirror, heart bouncing in his chest. "Dammit, he's following us. Could be plainclothes DEA." He tried to speak calmly, but heard a foreign, raspy sound spill out. "Get the map."

Too terrified to speak, Andy twisted in his seat to pull out the Rand McNally book that featured every dirt road in Maine. Dave accelerated. Andy dropped the map book and fumbled to pick it up, bumping his head against the glove compartment. The trailing car kept pace.

With a sudden right turn, Dave drove into the hidden back roads that had become familiar to him over the many months he'd spent here. Eventually, this would be a losing proposition for a sedan pursuing even a normal four-wheel-drive Blazer. But to Dave's surprise, the chase car persisted. He needed another plan.

"Take the wheel," Dave said. Andy slid over and waited for Dave to lift his butt off the seat. Within three seconds Andy was driving. From the passenger's seat, Dave studied the map as best he could on what had become a carnival ride, enduring intermittent blindness from intense flashes of sunlight through the trees.

It occurred to Dave that the game in this dirt-road maze could not go on forever. If Andy were caught, he couldn't be charged with anything. Nothing incriminating was in the car, and Andy didn't know much. Dave hated doing this to a new employee, but he needed to get away.

"Slow down at the next bend," Dave told Andy, who still had not spoken. "And then drive like hell."

Just before the next turn, Dave checked the lock, grabbed the handle, and set his jaw. They weren't too far from what he called a spit town—if you turned your head to spit, you might miss it—so he would have to walk a few miles. But he could find his way back.

Adrenaline pulsed through his temples. "Now!" Dave shouted, as much to himself as to Andy. He threw himself out of the truck, still moving at about thirty-five miles per hour. He fell and rolled down a steep, grassy knoll, and stayed perfectly still, not even swallowing until the chase car passed. Facedown, he made himself count to twenty before moving again, even when a large fly landed on his ear.

When he tried to stand, he stumbled and sat down until the spinning stopped. He dabbed his bloody nose with the back of a hand. Everything hurt. One thought saturated his consciousness: *I want my mother.*

Did he really just throw himself out of a moving vehicle in the middle of nowhere? What was he doing with his life? He was a college-educated man who had grown up in Coronado, married a nice girl and had a daughter, and could have been living a comfortable life, maybe selling insurance or real estate! There would be less money, sure. But at least he'd wake up every morning knowing what was going to happen. At least he'd be able to talk with his mother and sister.

Thinking of his sister made him flinch. Their relationship

was nonexistent now, given that she had become deputy district attorney in San Diego, and he was a fugitive. Talk about awkward. To communicate with his mother, he invented names for the various pay phones in Coronado. The one on First Street and Orange Avenue was Bill. Certain that authorities had tapped his mother's home phone, Dave would call her house from a pay phone and say, "See you at Bill's house in twenty minutes." He identified the booth at the Mobil station on Fourth Street and Orange Avenue with the name Alan. Dave knew the number for every pay phone in Coronado.

And then there was his wife, Linda, living by herself, essentially, in Denver. They went for weeks at a time with minimal communication. He didn't know how she put up with it. He felt like he'd become a terrible husband, father, son, and brother.

He would tell Lou tomorrow that he was out. No way could he keep doing this. Lou, Eddie, and Bob were partners, and earned far more than he did. Why wasn't he a partner, too? This wasn't worth it.

But first, he realized, he needed to find his way back to civilization. He steadied himself and dusted off his clothes. *Put one foot in front of the other,* he told himself. *Start walking.* As soon as he did, he tripped on an elevated root and fell down again, scraping his elbow and forehead. For a minute he considered staying there forever and wondered how long it would take his friends to find his decaying body. But late October brought a chill to the afternoon, which motivated an effort to pull himself up, cross his arms against the shivering, and spend the next few hours hiking. No, he thought to himself, "hiking" implied something pleasant, as though you were sightseeing, enjoying nature. Dave trudged until he found a one-pump gas station with a pay phone and called Fuzzy to pick him up.

News among the principals traveled fast. Joking attempted to cover the palpable anxiety. Andy, the new guy, had been caught and taken in. Apparently his back-roads driving skills fell short of Dave's. Andy wouldn't suffer too much. But that left a bigger problem: The silent ship full of hashish heading right for the Machias Bay cliff house, undoubtedly under surveillance. Dave tortured himself for not insisting on more discretion earlier in their residency. Of course the large house, with a bunch of guys coming and going, would attract attention from neighbors. It could only mean something illegal, unsavory, or just really weird.

Prosecutor Jim Brannigan had experience with both the state and federal government, and now worked in the US Attorney's office in Maine after a transfer from San Diego. Smuggling was not revolutionary in Maine, whose coastline and isolation practically advertised clandestine activity. The state was geographically large yet socially small, however, facilitating vigilance. Brannigan heard that local authorities had been looking into deeds for the most remote coastal houses that might host the growing smuggling trade they were trying to curtail, and found one registered to what looked like a shell business. It had no address beyond a PO box in Boston.

Obviously, law enforcement couldn't be everywhere. So they

asked a retired Swedish Secret Service agent who lived in the area to keep an eye on the house near Little Machias Bay; in doing so, the Swede arrested and questioned someone named Andy—low level and uncooperative. But Brannigan knew that nobody could operate off the wild coast of Maine alone.

After Dave's stuntman fiasco with Andy, the Little Machias Bay cliff house was deemed off-limits, prompting a tense gathering at the communications house. Dave nursed his cuts and scrapes, grumbled that all his clothes were at the other house, and called Lou to resign from the Company, only to have Lou talk him into staying in the sympathetic, paternal tone that made Dave forget the purpose of the conversation.

Eddie and Al bickered while waiting for word from the *Tusker*. Al insisted he had made contact, but Eddie thought Al was becoming delusional, inventing voices in the white noise. They couldn't just sit around, waiting for a ship full of illicit cargo to motor into the bay! If the radio wouldn't let them redirect the vessel to avoid a potential trap, they needed to locate it and communicate in person. Eddie knew he was the only one willing or able to do this.

Dave told Eddie he was insane, yelling that even if they knew the ship's course, it would be impossible. Eddie shouted back that if Dave had a better idea, he should give it a try. Dave sulked while Eddie stuffed an envelope full of Company money to execute the last resort.

Another suitcase. Another passport. Eddie flew to South Africa and chartered a plane. Given the amount of time that had passed, and the schedule that Dave had outlined for the ship to arrive at the end of December, Eddie started over the most logical patch in the Atlantic. Gripping binoculars and instructing the pilot to fly low in a systematic pattern the way a gardener would mow a lawn, Eddie searched. And searched. But thousands of square miles of ocean separated Cape Town and Maine. It would take an awful lot of good luck for him to pinpoint a 130-foot vessel and air-drop a desperate message the crew would find and interpret into the singular instruction: Go to a different location.

Dave had told Eddie he was insane, yelling that even if they knew the ship's course, it would be impossible. Eddie shouted back that if Dave had a better idea, he should give it a try. Dave sulked while Eddie spent Company money to execute what looked like a last resort.

On his third day in the air Eddie spotted two oil tankers and what he thought was a modern-day pirate ship. But not the *Tusker*. Eventually, he gave up and traveled back to the communications house in Maine, which was overflowing with dirty dishes and restless men.

Coronado Company crew members were assigned to watch Little Machias Bay from the other side of Cutler. Perched on a cliff in weather they grumbled was "colder than a witch's tit," they spotted the boat throwing out an anchor as dawn broke one morning—two weeks ahead of schedule. They scrambled to get word to Dave, who launched an effort to control the ensuing chaos.

The *Tusker* had encountered only one problem along the way: In the frigid North Atlantic waters between Maine and Nova

Scotia, the ship's antenna had frozen and broken off, leaving the captain with no way to reach Fuzzy and Al. But why not communicate earlier? Simply because he didn't want to hazard using the radio. In fact, encountering so few problems allowed the vessel to arrive early; Eddie later realized the reason why he could not locate the *Tusker* was because it had been farther north than his targeted area.

As soon as Dave sent two guys in a Zodiac to warn the *Tusker*, he considered calling Lou. Good old Lou, the mastermind who organized millions of dollars in deliveries and distribution, yet who always seemed to be on a lounge chair at the Beverly Hills Hotel or in Santa Barbara or Hilton Head or a hideaway he called "Rancho Relaxo" in Sun Valley when everything hit the fan, leaving Dave to clean up.

But he couldn't think about that now. Every minute counted. So he made a plan and started giving orders.

With the sun inching into the sky, the guys idled the Zodiac's motor just long enough to tell the captain to pull up his anchor and leave *now*. The metal claw had not even cracked the surface when everyone on board saw the Coast Guard in the distance. The Zodiac spun around and disappeared into a hidden inlet.

When the Coast Guard boarded the *Tusker*, they found nothing because the hatch to the hold, already in an unusual location, was shrouded in ice. Coast Guard officers ordered the *Tusker* to follow them back to port, but failed to leave an officer on board. The crew followed instructions with the speed of an errant child, languishing behind long enough to shatter the ice over the hatch and form a tight assembly line extracting the airtight containers and throwing them into the ocean. From a distant dock DEA agents spotted the frantic movement, heard shouting and the repeated *kerplunk* of thousands of pounds of hashish tumbling into the angry ocean, and realized what they'd missed.

Dave deployed people in every direction as he scrambled to escape Maine. In a desperate attempt to learn what was happening at the cliff house on Little Machias Bay, he sent Fuzzy to take a look. As soon as he did, Dave understood the mistake.

The police were waiting. Though Fuzzy would never talk, they collected what little they could find, which included torn pieces of phony identification and a business card. Later, when Jim Brannigan examined the materials, he took one look at the business card—*Philip DeMassa, Esq.*—and knew exactly what he'd found. The world wasn't so big, after all. It turned out that Brannigan had battled DeMassa a few times in San Diego courts and knew his reputation well. While the law enforcement team also had Don Kidd, and several others, in custody, dramatic captures did not always yield enough evidence for prosecutions. Brannigan knew this as well as anyone.

Chapter 26

1979

SHAKEN, DAVE ACCEPTED LOU'S INVITATION TO JOIN him and Kerrie in the newly completed guesthouse on Lou's property at Palmetto Dunes in Hilton Head, South Carolina. Not a mansion, exactly, but impressive nonetheless. Lou's renovations included a tennis court, pool, hot tub, and lounge chairs on a wooden deck secluded with trees and shrubbery, overlooking the white sand beach.

The luxurious surroundings could not hide the reality: the last year of the decade had started poorly. Dave was torn between gratitude for the schedule (drinks at five o'clock) and fierce resentment. He imagined Lou receiving massages in a spa at a five-star hotel while he left part of his soul in Maine.

Dave always described Kerrie as "delightful," but he noticed that the once friendly girl had changed. She kept to herself, avoided interactions, and could not cover the dark circles under her eyes. Dave guessed that living on the run, no matter what your lifestyle, unsettled everyone at some point.

"I talked to Phil," Lou said, pouring a glass of wine from a Riedel decanter. "Looks like ten people are in custody, but most of them don't know anything."

"Except for Fuzzy." Dave's hand shook as he brought the glass to his lips. He guessed it would take months to calm his nerves.

"They won't talk. A little extra money won't hurt either."

Dave said nothing. He could not wrap his mind around the dollars that went out the door to purchase silence, buy out former partners, secure Phil DeMassa's legal expertise, and patch up blunders.

Kerrie passed through without speaking to either one of them, and sat on the comforter in the bedroom, staring at the floor. From his vantage point, Dave could see the haggard expression on her once soft, appealing face. He looked at Lou and raised his eyebrows in Kerrie's direction.

Lou shook his head but said nothing.

"Are you two okay?" Dave asked.

From the other room Kerrie shouted, "No, Dave, we're not okay." She marched out and stood at the end of the living room with one hand planted on a hip. "He lies to me all the time. I love him, but we have no life. I'm almost thirty years old and I want to get married and have kids and use my real freaking name!" Then she looked at Lou. "I love you with all my heart. But the strange thing is, even after all these years, I'm not sure I even know you."

As she turned back to the bedroom, Kerrie mumbled, "When

I die, I want people to say more about me than, 'Wow, she had a great tan.'" Then she slammed the door.

"I've never seen her like this." Dave set down his drink. "Want me to talk to her?"

"No." Lou shook his head. "She's a good one, but . . ."

"But what?"

"I suppose every relationship has a shelf life. And other factors don't help." He gulped his drink. "Come on. Let's finish this business and relax by the pool. We were talking about some hush money."

This hurled Dave back into accounting mode. "The problem is, we invested a lot in this last deal: planes, boats, high-tech gear, and I don't even know what else. You should take a look at the books. And we lost the entire shipment. Over a million dollars dumped into the water!"

"Well, at least the DEA had to share it with some fishermen."

"Glad you can joke about it. But I'm tired of moving one step forward, three steps back. You're never there. You don't know what it's like to jump out of a car and roll around in the dirt and hike for miles."

"David." Lou moved to sit down on the couch beside Dave and softened his tone. "It's not the end of the world, my friend. They don't have a single Company partner. This is why Phil DeMassa works for us."

Dave looked away and sipped wine, sighed, then turned back to Lou. While still trim, for the most part, Lou was carrying a few more pounds than he had in his younger days. Impossible to avoid with this lifestyle, where you almost felt compelled to spend the money when it appeared. Lou wore (yet another) pricey shirt in the latest style (which still meant expansive collars), a gold chain, and a longer, curlier hairstyle—possibly an attempt to hide the receding hairline. A touch of gray crept through the temples, and a thick mustache covered his upper lip. It might have seemed to Dave that Lou removed himself from the stress, but he could tell from new lines etched at the corners of Lou's eyes that years running from the law, fleeing the inevitability they all felt just below the surface, were aging him, too.

"Do me a favor." Lou was not asking a question. "Burn the accounting records."

"I usually do that after the job is finished."

"Make an exception this time."

"We should stop," Dave said. "Please. Let's get out. Together. I have a family now, Lou. A daughter—who has a father who can't even keep his names straight, who doesn't even know what to call his friends. Who are you now? C. R. Richards?"

Lou inhaled slowly, trying to remain impassive. "Depends on where I am. I use a different name for each part of the country. And world, I suppose. That's how I keep them straight."

"Until you accidentally leave a bunch of fake IDs in the San Francisco Hyatt."

Lou shuddered at the mention of his careless slipup—right in Union Square! He couldn't even remember when it had happened, but he faintly recalled the story he had given to hotel security— something about being a wealthy businessman having an affair, needing to conceal his identity as Richard Bentley, who came from an important family, of course.

In truth, exiting the business crossed Lou's mind every day. With the cash on hand and the sale of his properties, he could live in some foreign land quite comfortably. He knew Kerrie wouldn't join him. It was unfortunate, but he was tired of the emotional roller coaster some of her new pastimes induced. Plus, her demand for intimacy and a traditional life—marriage, kids, and one home with a neighborhood and social life—had gone from enlightening to taxing. He wanted to keep her safe; the less she knew the better. It would be easier to get a beach house in the Bahamas and find an island girl who wouldn't ask so many questions and expect so much out of life. Strong women were electrifying. And tiring.

But he shared none of these thoughts with Dave. Instead, he confronted his former student and trusted friend: "If you stopped, what would you do? And what would I do without you?"

"I don't know, but we should get out now, while we can. We can't run forever."

"You can't leave me, David." Lou placed a hand on Dave's knee, for emphasis. "Just a little longer. Then we'll have everything we need for the rest of our lives. I promise."

The phone rang, piercing the silence. Kerrie answered and marched into the living room. "That was Mike Agnor. *Again.* You need to pay him."

Lou exhaled and said to Dave, "Contractors. For our renovations."

"Lou owes fifty-five thousand dollars and won't pay them," Kerrie said. "It's so rude."

"I'll pay. I told them we lost a lot of money, and they have to wait a little longer."

Dave straightened. "You said *we lost money*? What else did you tell them?"

Lou averted his gaze. "That's not important."

"Yeah, right," Kerrie mumbled before grabbing her purse and sunglasses, and slamming the front door behind her.

"Lou, what are you doing? Everyone loves her. And she's good for you. She has . . . character, fortitude. And it looks like she's going to leave."

"She already told me she's leaving. Says she deserves better. I guess she does."

"But you don't seem to care."

"Of course I care. But I think this is the natural evolution of things. You can't stay close to people outside the business."

Dave tried to absorb this information, which made Lou seem uncharacteristically dismissive. Maybe the years had hardened him. Or maybe Lou was just stating a simple fact. Dave tried again: "What did you tell your contractors about losing money?"

"I didn't say anything. We're just a few high rollers at the blackjack table—who lost millions. People sense that."

"So . . . we should leave the table!"

Lou laughed. "Not us. That's when we start planning the next deal to replace the loss. We have a choice. We can cower and hide like losers. Or we can find our way back to the ranks of the most talented and lucrative smugglers in the world." Lou raised his glass. "To the power of choice."

Dave realized he would not change Lou's mind. So he murmured, "Choice." But even as the wine danced along his tongue, he marveled at how every time a choice presented itself, he made the wrong one. Or more profoundly, he wondered if he were in so deep now that choices amounted to little more than mirages.

"Trust me, David. This is nothing but a minor setback in the middle of a tough game. But we're a winning team." Lou leaned toward Dave, lowering his voice. "And winners don't quit."

Brannigan shared his information with the DEA on the East Coast, who contacted Jim Conklin in his office. The DEA was still new enough, communication and triangulation still unsophisticated enough, that regional groups often operated in isolation. More art than science, Nixon's war on drugs had taken on many colors and shades since he had left office, and while the mission was clear, the method sometimes resembled a kindergarten finger painting.

But Conklin, a New Yorker at heart, hated boredom. And this case intrigued him. He knew it was bigger than the low priority the office assigned to it. The "kiddie dope" label did not help either. Bobby Dunne had believed in it, as did Conklin's associate, Special Agent Larry McKinney, a slim, no-nonsense man with a beard and wide forehead who often dressed in suits that looked a size too big for him. Conklin had no intention of letting it fade into the background. The fact that a night out for Conklin and his colleagues amounted to one-drink appetizer specials at El Torito after a twelve-hour workday made the prospect of taking down outlaws—who lived a life of ease and luxury that hardworking guys like Conklin could only imagine—even more enticing.

In the industrial park setting south of Coronado, Conklin set down a cardboard box of long-awaited office supplies. He unfurled a world map Dunne had left, and mounted it on the bulletin board. Conklin stood for a minute, rubbing his mustache before selecting a few brightly colored pushpins from the just-opened plastic container. Then he grinned, and started decorating the coast of Maine.

Chapter 27

1980

AFTER BARELY ESCAPING MAINE AND LEAVING several guys in custody, Dave continued to yearn for a normal life. A tie-wearing, clock-punching, Volvo-driving, family-growing existence notably absent of angst. But Lou always pulled him back. Each conversation finished with an extra coating of Lou's singular charm, sprinkled with mentor/coach encouragement. The predictability made it no less enticing, the promises no less desirable: more autonomy and responsibility, more importance and respect, more money, more friendship and acceptance, more love.

At three o'clock in the morning, Dave bolted upright in bed, drenched in sweat from the nightmares that continued to haunt him. The details varied, but the core always involved a Company boat sinking, authorities swooping in, people he cared about getting hurt or dying. Smuggling gone wrong, with the failure pressing on his shoulders. The insomnia frayed him from his burning eyes to his jittery fingertips.

Yet instead of running back to his wife and daughter and cozy home and life with one identity that he could actually remember, Dave found himself doing reconnaissance from a chartered Cessna over Neah Bay on the Olympic Peninsula in Washington State, charting the details for the biggest load yet: ten tons of Thai sticks, with help from fellow smuggler "Little Ricky" Bibbero via Bob Lahodny, a new boat, and a helicopter or two. The expected payday? More than $30 million.

A former army helicopter pilot named Hugo Butz helped Dave secure a pilot, navigator, and mechanic out of Fort Lewis for the off-load. They agreed to sneak out a double-rotor Chinook (*A few hours in the middle of the night, tops. Who will notice?*), fly to the vessel, and transport the cargo to a patch of land cleared by logging. This would allow the boat to stay several miles offshore, and (hopefully) avoid the potential traps and pitfalls closer to the beach.

Dave faced two problems: making sure the helicopter could carry the load safely, and the absence of his regulars. After the indictment and the close call in Maine, Don Kidd had priced himself out of participation, demanding more money and offering less time for his mechanical brilliance. Dave found a new tech geek who fulfilled his needs for bugs and anything else that would help him keep tabs on a crew he wasn't sure he could trust.

Dave knew this was their chance to make up for the *Tusker*, but the nightmares fueled perpetual anxiety (or maybe it was the other way around). New faces didn't help. The only time he felt halfway normal was when he articulated plans, buried phone numbers in complex multiplication codes, ran budgets, or calculated distance and time and profits.

Everything seemed organized on a hot summer night in August, chosen for its agreeable conditions. The *John L. Winter*, a cargo ship with many miles and even more layers of rust, arrived on time. The onshore crew was ready with the necessary equipment, including hundreds of gallons of extra fuel for the helicopter.

But a cold, dense fog enveloped the entire coast. The Northwest was not Southern California, Dave realized. Ever. For a moment he just wished he could go back to swimming bales through the surf, where the worst complication was a rogue set or a tangled leash. Where his name was Dave and not Doug Morton or Wayne Rothchild or Yancy Farquhar, and he was able to communicate with his music. Point A to point B, and that was it. A few bucks, vodka with a hint of triple sec, a teriyaki chicken dinner at the Chart House, a few laughs, a lifetime ago.

He had orchestrated the construction of a custom collapsible cage, or cargo net, aboard the *John L. Winter*. The lift would cinch the top of the netting, providing structure during the flight to the designated landing place. This would occur two or three times until all ten tons were in the U-Hauls waiting to carry the product to the Company's latest distribution center.

But the weather changed everything. The helicopter couldn't

leave Fort Lewis. Nor was the pilot (who seemed to reconsider his pursuit of "easy" money) eager to reschedule, given the increased security the base had recently implemented. Meanwhile, the ship's captain complained about running out of food and water, along with his growing vulnerability while everyone waited for the fog to clear.

Frantic, Dave called Lou, who was not about to let this shipment get away. Lou's inability to abide by any kind of personal budget for nearly a decade had taken a toll. He spent whatever he wanted, owned approximately thirty luxury cars and several houses, traveled first class, stayed in five-star hotels, and didn't look at the bill when he checked out. Now he felt constrained. The contractors on his Hilton Head house hounded him. Phil DeMassa demanded $40,000 and $50,000 every time he opened a file. But what could Lou do? Fire DeMassa? The consigliere who "owned" Bob Lahodny's Santa Barbara estate, everyone's favorite gathering place? Who laundered the money in all sorts of subtle, savvy ways? Who helped them master hiding in high society? Nope, the attorney had Lou by the balls.

All Lou ever wanted was the ease of not having to worry about money. How had it come to this? Now, for the first time since those early days in Mexico, a compulsion drew him back to the trenches, where he hoped some reasoning and sophistication would change the course of this delivery. He chartered a plane, piloted by Butz, and flew to Olympia, Washington.

Lou met with everyone at the Red Lion Inn, infusing a combination of affability, threats, and enthusiasm into the discussion. Everything seemed set. Lou shook hands, bought a round of drinks, and excused himself "for just a moment." He never returned.

When the weather finally cleared, the helicopter didn't show, and the pilot phoned in enough excuses to make Dave realize that he needed to enact another plan. Immediately.

Following Lou's lead, Eddie traveled from Santa Barbara to the preparation and distribution center, situated in an old barn.

"We're screwed," Dave mumbled. "The pilot bailed out again."

"We got this," Eddie said. "We'll go back to what we know best: Zodiacs, barges, four-wheel drives. Everything's here."

"We can't fit ten tons on one barge, so it'll take a couple of trips." Dave paused. "The captain said something about an Indian Reservation. Makah, I think. Fisherman, so they always have boats. It's right there. What do you think?"

At dawn Eddie ventured into the Makah Indian Reservation adjacent to Neah Bay, cash in hand, as he'd done before in so many ports. But the negotiations on this tiny slice of land in Washington proved trickier than Mexico, Morocco, Thailand, Singapore, Pakistan, or South Africa. Or maybe Eddie revealed desperation he'd never felt before. He knew what this deal meant to Lou. To all of them. With the exception of real estate investments, not a single one had managed the money he'd earned. The assumption was that it would keep flowing. So they kept spending.

When Eddie reported that the Makah Indians wanted $150,000, Dave buried his face in his hands and swore. But they had spent the entire day gathering gear and begging for help, and couldn't wait any longer: Either the captain would leave with their product, or the Coast Guard would catch them.

When the tide was where they wanted it, turmoil reigned. Radio etiquette disappeared; multiple people spoke at once, dropping codes and reducing Dave to yelling as if he were trying to control a wayward classroom. He watched through his night-vision scope as his crew scurried to and fro, accomplishing nothing. Why was nobody following directions? Eddie was gone, having departed as quickly as he'd appeared. Someone was trying to manage the Indians, who ignored orders if they thought their boats might get damaged. An hour and a half passed.

Then it started to rain. The view through his scope smeared, but not enough to prevent Dave from seeing the surf pick up. Logic had told him that a north-facing beach in the summer would remain relatively calm. But then again, every body of water and shoreline came with its own personality—and sense of humor. Dave contemplated leaving the perch on the hill that allowed him to spot problems. He glanced at his watch again. They were now almost three hours behind schedule. He closed his eyes and tried to calm himself.

More squawking and useless communication poured from the radios. The only way around the surf was through a nearby tributary. But it was passable only with a high tide. At low tide, the ground swallowed boats. And the tide, unfortunately, showed no mercy for their inefficiencies. The sky began to shed its inky blackness, a curtain rising in slow motion. In a matter of minutes, the river became too shallow, and the Indians knew it. They beached their boats, unloaded whatever cargo they had carried, and nodded good-bye.

But the job was not done. The barge was still out there, carrying millions of dollars' worth of Thai stick.

Fuzzy, released on bail after his arrest in Maine, announced that he would go. He drove the Zodiac out through the waves, landing with an audible thud in each trough, until he reached the thirty-five-foot-long Kevlar barge stacked with bales. He hooked the two vessels together and started pulling in the heavy cargo. "I got it, I got it!" Fuzzy shouted over the radio to Dave, who swallowed hard when he saw the *John L. Winter* pull its anchor and fire its engines—with about $10 million of shipment that would undoubtedly get tossed overboard.

As the Zodiac strained toward shore, Fuzzy felt the rope go slack. He looked back and saw an enormous wave—maybe eight or ten feet—lift the Kevlar barge and hurl it toward him. Fuzzy punched the motor. But it wasn't enough. The front of the barge submerged the back of the Zodiac, pinning him to the floor and swamping the boat. But his hand was still on the throttle, and a lifetime around engines told him to give this one every last bit of gas. The water shifted and the motor screamed, propelling the Zodiac out from under the barge. The line broke. Fuzzy raced the whitewash toward shore, closely followed by bales of Thai stick and the Kevlar barge tumbling across an irate ocean.

Dave ran down the hill to make sure Fuzzy and the beach crew lived through the ordeal and carried what they could to the waiting U-Haul box truck. The seabirds and sun announced the team's greatest danger: a clear day. And the preparation and repackaging center was still ten miles away.

Dave knew that the beginning of a gig set the tone for the entire night. Sure enough, this one never recovered. A heavily loaded U-Haul was not supposed to be on this uneven, mud-soaked road—the only way out of the enclave. Nobody had scouted it. They were down to plan D-minus at this point. So even as Dave shouted at the driver to move slowly out of the area to avoid getting stuck, the truck fishtailed and swerved to a stop at a forty-five-degree angle in the mire. At that point, Dave did not even have the energy to swear.

He thought about trying to use one of the other four-by-fours to pull it out, but it looked like a more appropriate job for the Chinook helicopter. "Move as much as you can to the pickups," Dave instructed, knowing they were already full. "Everything that'll fit."

"The whole frame's bent!" Fuzzy shouted while struggling with the door. "We gotta break it!"

But, alas, the emergency list did not include an ax. They kept trying—to no avail. And then Dave realized that all the bad luck (not to mention the yelling, noise, and general pandemonium during a covert operation) presented another choice: increase their risk of getting caught with every passing minute, or take what they had in the pick-ups and abandon the rest.

"Wipe it down and leave it. Move *slowly* until you get to the main road!" Dave could not believe he was announcing a code red; even as he said it, he knew they'd left fingerprints on the inside. Yet another mistake. In a flurry of activity, the crew wiped every outside surface they had touched, piled into the Chevy trucks, and drove away from the multimillion-dollar Coronado Company yard sale.

What a disaster, Dave thought, as he ran the numbers in his head. They could salvage just enough to pay the investors. Then again, the principals might need to dip into their own pockets to close the deal. Between the investment required to stage this shipment and the loss of the last one, their record was closer to one step forward, five steps back.

Now he *really* wanted out. But how could he leave after this?

As they turned onto the paved road, Dave rolled down the window to get some air. Just thinking about the conversation he would have with Lou made him sick to his stomach.

Chapter 28

1980

JIM CONKLIN COVERED THE PHONE RECEIVER AND hollered to anyone who would listen: "Coronado PD got another one! They're bringing him here."

In the DEA offices, they all gathered around a metal table that tipped slightly whenever someone rested on it because one leg was shorter than the others. Or the floor was warped. A young man in his twenties stared at his shoes, his shoulders shaking. He leaned on the table, felt it pitch, then removed his elbows with a start.

One glance told Conklin that the kid wouldn't last a week in jail.

"You're in a bind here, son." Conklin saw no need for initial niceties. "Dealing drugs on the street is a felony, and it looks like we caught you in the act with some pretty fancy Thai stick, which isn't too common in Coronado. So you know, that whole 'alleged' thing really goes out the window. You follow me?" Conklin looked at the Coronado Police Department report. "You hear what I'm saying?"

The young man's gaze remained on his tennis shoes—one with the laces filthy and untied, the other with empty eyelets. He nodded slightly.

"Right. Let's make sure you understand your options here." Over the next twenty minutes Conklin worked his magic, playing hard-ass cop, disappointed father, and sympathetic buddy with the aptitude of Robert De Niro. "Let me boil it down: Give us something, or go to jail."

"I know someone," the young man blurted. "Me, I'm nobody. But this guy, he's big-time. If I tell you his name, can I go?"

"The deal doesn't work with just a name," Conklin said. "But I'll tell you what. Start with all the information you got, and I'll give you my word that we can work something out."

"I won't go to jail?"

"Not if you give us something we can use."

The dealer wiped his nose. "Eddie Otero. Calls himself James Norris. I think. Sometimes. Or Kenneth Eugene Cook. Junior. He's got a lotta names."

Conklin worked to control his excitement. "Where'd you cross paths with him?"

"Coronado. And Santa Barbara."

Huh, Conklin thought, sitting back in his chair. Up the coast in a town that represented a huge geographical gap in the DEA's coverage, and an easy place to blend in with lots of money and an affinity for the beach. These guys were no dummies. But he already knew that. "Where?"

"At his house. Like, in the hills, for a party or something? Cima Linda? Don't remember the number. But I could say how it looks. The house. Where we partied." He sniffed again.

"How do I know you're not bullshitting me?"

"'Cause . . . I'm his cousin and I know stuff!" He slumped into the chair, his brow furrowed in remorse. "That enough?"

Conklin declared that they would finish the conversation in the car, on the way to Santa Barbara. Four hours later they found the house, but nobody was home and Conklin didn't have a warrant. A quick follow-up at the Montecito Post Office showed that a forwarding address (so mail didn't pile up when Eddie traveled?) belonged to a woman named Bambi Merryweather. *Sounds like a stripper,* Conklin thought. Back in San Diego he started to cross-reference Merryweather and Otero and the rumored aliases in the DEA's nascent database. Flagged.

He called someone on the East Coast to compare notes. Yes, they were looking into a Bambi Merryweather, a former model who might be tied to a suspected drug smuggler in Hilton Head, South Carolina, possibly fetching mail there, too. *How did they make these connections?* Conklin asked.

Through contractors in Hilton Head. Mike and Jerry Agnor, brothers and business partners, were fed up with a client's belligerent refusal to pay. So they sent letters to the person he claimed was his secretary: Bambi Merryweather.

The Agnors continued to confront the client, C. R. Richards, who finally told them he couldn't pay because he'd lost millions of dollars in two drug shipments gone awry. *Don't you know who I am?* He boasted of his prowess as the preeminent drug smuggler in the United States, with global connections who would do anything for him. The Agnors didn't appreciate the attempt at intimidation. So they reported him to the local authorities.

Conklin arranged to meet them in San Diego, and walked through the entire book of names and pictures he'd assembled from the indictment.

Crisply dressed and speaking with a southern drawl that sounded foreign in the California office, the Agnors picked out pictures of Louis Villar—one from *The Beachcomber*, the Coronado High School yearbook, and another shot with lighter, curlier hair. They also mentioned an accountant in San Diego named Andrew Willis, who handled Villar's finances. Conklin made a note to investigate Mr. Willis, considering how this might allow him to change the frame, recruit the Internal Revenue Service, and present it as an asset case. When you wanted to catch criminals dirty but couldn't ensnare them in the act, flagging their teacher or lifeguard salaries and the inexplicable acquisition of luxury homes, cars, boats, travel, and watches could offer a promising alternative.

Remaining fugitives for years, as Lou Villar, Eddie Otero, and Bob Lahodny had managed, took some level of proficiency and care. And Conklin knew Villar was the most cautious of them all. His only weaknesses seemed to be flashy cars and too many women (though they all were devoted enough, apparently, to

231

keep quiet). But now he was telling the Agnor brothers, who looked like they'd stepped right out of church, that he couldn't or wouldn't pay them the fifty grand he owed because of a drug deal gone wrong? Bragging that he was a kingpin, and if they knew what was good for them, they'd wait patiently or go away?

This signaled a major change, but not an unpredictable one. That's what he loved about this business. While these guys were among the most competent and creative he'd ever come across— geniuses, in some respects, or at least visionaries—even the most intelligent drug smugglers imploded. Like Macbeth, their hubris and ambition and addiction to the rush always got the better of them. Agents called it "weed greed."

Conklin considered the human folly that could creep into the DEA office, where everyone was driven by a deep sense of right and wrong and duty to his country: affairs, collapsing marriages, alcohol you could still smell in the morning, the occasional gambling addiction. He compared it with the world of smuggling, where the players were driven by personal gain with no regard for the law or anyone their actions affected, yet their lives depended on the validity of their word, their honesty as businessmen. He shuffled it around in his mind until everything fell back into cogent categories of good and evil.

Chapter 29

1981

LOU AND DAVE ARRIVED AT BOB'S SANTA BARBARA estate, protected by high walls and acres of gardens and trees on Ashley Road in Montecito, not far from Lou's and Eddie's homes. Bob said good-bye to the tennis pro he'd hired for himself, and strolled into the house dressed in a white V-neck sweater and white shorts, toweling his forehead and the avant-garde fuzz he'd grown on his chin. He greeted Lou and Dave while house staff arranged flowers in a large vase and fetched beverages for everyone.

A thundering engine navigating the curved driveway to the parking area around the fountain signaled the unmistakable arrival of a Ferrari. Eddie marched through the front door like the house was his own and announced, "Man, I always feel like the sheik of Arabeek when I come into this place!"

"What are you even talking about?" Dave's irritation had soared the minute he'd heard the Ferrari. He thought Eddie drove it just to taunt him; everyone knew it had been a Christmas present from Lou.

"Dave!" The friendly greeting annoyed Dave even more. How was Eddie always so oblivious? Happy? Surrounded by friends?

Lou started right in: "First, I want an update on Lance. I don't like what I'm hearing."

Eddie sat down in a leather armchair. "Still trying to get the boat business going in Tahoe."

"The cigarette boats he's trying to sell are too double-oh-seven for any normal use," Bob said. "They're even too much for us! That's why the business is failing."

Lou nodded. "He builds what he wants instead of understanding what consumers need. I heard he's still making a scene, speeding and shooting up rooster tails. He just can't help himself."

"He can't keep his flippin' mouth shut either," Dave interjected.

"I tried to tell him," Eddie said.

"Showing off is a fatal flaw," Dave announced. Then he looked around at Lou, who owned multiple houses and too many cars to count; Bob, who resided on an estate a famous movie star would struggle to afford, replete with stables for his prized polo ponies; and Eddie, who regularly clocked more than one hundred miles per hour along Highway 101 in his Ferrari and stumbled out of the Santa Barbara Polo & Racquet Club every week. Meanwhile, here sat Dave, driving the same old Chevy Blazer, keeping everything low-key, but unable to encourage moderation in his superiors. Then again, people didn't risk their lives and freedom because they were interested in moderation. He decided to keep quiet.

"You think he'll turn?" Lou asked.

"No." Eddie shrugged. "But you've known him longer than me. Buying him out was like the Steve Miller Band paying off Steve Miller to leave!"

"I'm not sure that's relevant, Eddie," Lou said. "But you know we didn't have a choice. Still, Lance has to be getting desperate. I'm heading over to my psychic again this afternoon. I'll ask her."

"Oh," Eddie said. "Okay. That's cool." Everybody else pretended they had not heard their leader of nearly a decade admit that he would once again seek direction from a crystal ball or tarot cards. They preferred to believe that Lou's psychic was his own "Deep Throat," a source of perplexing yet essential information.

"I've given this a lot of thought, and I believe it's time for us to get out," Lou continued. "We've pushed our luck; Eddie and I are at the top of the DEA's list right now."

Everyone nodded solemnly. Ice settled in Dave's glass.

"But first, we need one more big barbecue." Lou smiled, trying to summon the charm that had motivated student-athletes in years past. "We can't retire like this! With two major failures and debt. Besides, unemployment's on the way up again, and the country's in a major recession. And it's only going to get worse. Just one more, the way we've always done it, on familiar territory. Not overly ambitious. So we can live comfortably. Call it . . . a recovery run."

The reference to the failures and debt resulting from the debacles in Maine and Washington made Dave reach for a glass of water, sip, swallow wrong, cough uncontrollably, then sink into his chair. The room fell silent.

"We have a choice," Lou said. "We need everyone for this. So what's it going to be?"

They looked at the floor. Dave's voice cracked: "We could disappear again. It might be smart to try to stay out of trouble."

A gardener's lawn mower started up in a distant acre of Bob's yard. A decorative grandfather clock ticked.

Eddie thought about the danger. But the boredom he and Bob felt, loomed larger. He had traveled the world, and enjoyed all the real estate, cars, watches, parties, alcohol, and women a man could manage. What was left for him to do? His voice tore through the quiet: "Go big or go home! I'm in."

Dave refrained from commenting, but knew Eddie would be "in" if Lou announced they were going to blow up the house and see if they could get out in time, just for fun. The guy didn't have the sense to be afraid of anything. And yet, aside from the arguments and tense moments between them, he admitted that Eddie had always watched out for him.

Bob nodded. "I'm in." He agreed to work with Little Ricky Bibbero and arrange for a load of high-quality Thai grass. He also mentioned a contract opportunity—taking a percentage for assisting with execution—for a summer delivery at Hollister Ranch, in the Santa Barbara area.

But their main focus would be their own shipment, slated for October. For that, Eddie would collect the down payment from investors, make sure the money got to the right places, and solidify transport.

Torn between an insatiable desire to redeem himself and the

need to have a normal life while it still might be possible, Dave didn't answer. But Lou made the presumptive close, telling Dave to work with the accountant, Andrew Willis, to determine their resources and budget. While Dave was at it, Lou added, maybe he could convince Willis to invest too?

They decided to return to Bear Harbor, hidden in Sinkyone Wilderness State Park on the Lost Coast of California. Familiarity required minimal scouting. Without ever saying yes, Dave was in with the rest of them.

Over the next couple of months they made plans at Lou's house. After Kerrie had moved out, he had returned to his wild ways, and now lived with two sisters who lounged on a large opium bed in the living room, sketching pictures of waves and sunsets, orchids, or Native American dream catchers while watching their shared lover, Lou, smoke a cigar or drink wine as he oversaw one last epic deal.

Instead of going for ten tons again, they would behave more sensibly and reduce it to five. To ensure control throughout the journey, Eddie used his own money to purchase the *Robert Wayne* and hire the captain. Everyone knew the danger had grown exponentially, but they sold the idea to one another—and themselves—the same way: just one more time.

Soon the ship began its months-long journey from Thailand to California.

Chapter 30

1981

EVERY FEW WEEKS JIM CONKLIN DROVE FOUR hours up to Santa Barbara with a crew of agents. By day they watched the various houses, kept an eye out for Ferraris and Mercedes 6.9s, and waited for the Coronado Company to emerge from the swank Chanticleer Restaurant while the DEA agents ate out of vending machines or Styrofoam. Whoever didn't have the night shift grabbed a drink at Joe's Café on State Street. With such a tight budget, they stayed in the cheapest motels, with some sleeping on the floor. A couple of guys decided it was more comfortable to snooze in the car and did that instead. They waited. Conklin was infinitely clear: They would watch, but not pounce until they had enough evidence. It had been almost four years since the indictment. The last thing they needed was to put the Coronado Company on notice so the fugitives could disappear for another four.

Back in San Diego, Conklin silently thanked accountant Andrew Willis for his diligent record keeping and slack disposal methods. Clandestine rounds with the local trash collectors, with special attention to the rubbish from Andrew Willis's office (a warrant was unnecessary if the garbage was outside of curtilage, the bubble around your private property), revealed a wide world of aliases, shell companies, bank accounts in faraway places, and property held in various names. This included a multimillion-dollar estate supposedly owned by Phil DeMassa, whose name seemed to slither across the desk of every San Diego DEA agent at one time or another. But Conklin was so enthusiastic about the flow of information that whenever he started a new file, he told their new secretary that he wanted to punch the letters on the label maker himself.

Bad news reached Eddie. The *Robert Wayne* was in trouble, making distress calls to the Philippines. Something about a rogue wave. The propeller shaft broke, leaving the ship adrift and loaded with tons of illegal drugs. The captain, who remained in port, having sent his first mate on the journey, sought help from his sister. She was an escort at an Australian bar in Tokyo, where, as a six-feet-tall blonde who had been blind since birth, she earned $1,000 a night from the yakuza, a multinational organized crime syndicate operating out of Japan. In hushed, smoke- and sake-filled rooms on the outskirts of Tokyo, they agreed to help the Company avoid calling the Coast Guard and to oversee the cargo during the ship's repairs. *But you know,* they reminded their favorite Amazon-like escort, *that type of support isn't free*. The *Robert Wayne* had already called for help, increasing everyone's exposure. The price tag for this special assistance? $300,000.

Nobody but Eddie could deliver the money. But he also needed to direct funds toward repairing the ship, now estimated at $250,000. So there would be two trips.

Eddie secured an advance from an investor, then carried the trusty French luggage, with its secret compartments loaded with cash, to meet the yakuza on Chichi Jima, about five hundred miles off the coast of Japan. There they could dry-dock the *Robert Wayne* for repairs. For good measure, the yakuza demanded that Eddie stay with them until the rest of the money came through. But he finally convinced them that he was the only person who could actually bring the funds. So they let him go.

When he returned, he stayed until the ship was ready to sail.

Wary of the annihilated budget and the premonition that yet another shipment of Thai sticks would sleep with the fishes, Dave tracked the *Robert Wayne* as it seemed to putter toward California.

The off-load into Bear Harbor was mercifully uneventful. Most of the dispensation had been set up in advance, translating to rapid returns to investors and the yakuza, which Eddie conveyed as fast as the cash came to him.

When Lou ordered Dave to shut down the distribution house to reduce costs, Dave was unsure about what to do with the rest of the cargo. A jubilant-sounding Lou said to him, "Don't worry about it. Bring it back to my house in Santa Barbara."

"Really?" Dave said into the pay phone. "You've never done anything like that."

"It's just a few days, until the rest of the distribution confirmations come through. Plus, I want to show the girls. We need to celebrate."

"Lou, it's nine hundred pounds. We could extend the lease on the barn, and leave some up here. There's a lot of cash, too. Maybe you want to put in the Hong Kong account?"

"No, I want to keep an eye on it. Record everything, like always. Then shut it down. Bob's throwing a victory party for us, and you won't want to miss it! By the way, I've decided that you deserve a gift for your hard work. You got us back on track. I want to thank you for a job well done."

After all they had endured, an irrepressible smile illuminated Dave's face. But he kept his voice even. "Yeah, I wouldn't want to miss the festivities. I'll see you soon."

On November 5, Conklin and his team were back in Santa Barbara living like impoverished students, debating between spending money on gas or food. The annual government budget had been used up (sometimes it happened as early as September), but they weren't about to alter their plans to wait for new funds. It had taken a lot to get to this point, to gather enough evidence. So they opened their wallets and moved ahead. Conklin placed his agents around Montecito and Hillcrest, and waited.

A Mercedes returning from a pickup at the airport was on the move, turning west on Alston Road. Conklin asked the agent to read him the license plate again, then told the others stationed nearby to confirm the driver and passengers before following.

Eddie and Bob had just retrieved Dave from the Santa Barbara airport for an accounting meeting. From the backseat, Dave noticed a worker stationed high on a wooden pole near a Pacific Telephone truck, talking on a walkie-talkie, looking toward Eddie's car. Then he saw a woman pushing a baby carriage, also staring at them. Cops? Or was he just paranoid?

"Does anything seem off to you guys?" Dave asked.

"What?" asked Bob. "No. We're all good. It's a beautiful day!"

"You want some music, Dave?" Eddie turned up Blondie singing "The Tide is High."

But Dave knew their success as fugitives in Santa Barbara had made Eddie and Bob complacent. He placed his hand on the manila folder sitting next to him. Receipts and ledgers from the most recent gig, plus a few fake California driver's licenses, were organized neatly inside. Dave kept each slip of paper until they settled the books, when they ceremoniously burned everything in a fire and drank champagne. But here he was, he realized, traveling with a whole lot of evidence. And cash.

Now who was the complacent one?

A minute later they turned onto Cima Linda Road, where the meeting was set to take place, and a group of DEA, FBI, and IRS agents greeted them with guns drawn.

Eddie held his breath. He could not believe it had come to

this. After twelve years of the most treacherous circumstances in Mexico, Thailand, Pakistan, India, Morocco, South Africa, Chichi Jima (and other places nobody had ever heard of), Maine, Washington, and every inch of California, a thousand hours in the air and on boats in faraway oceans, and a thousand more in the surf on a Zodiac or with a bundle tied to him, tumbling on the waves, finding his aptitude for bargaining, thriving in danger, feeling needed, appreciated, important, and rich, now here he was: getting caught in his Mercedes on the way to an accounting meeting in the suburbs.

Gesturing with their weapons, the agents yelled at Eddie, Bob, and Dave to step out of the car. They placed handcuffs on Eddie and Bob, their main targets. They didn't identify Dave immediately, so amid the yelling and confusion, he attempted to retrieve his briefcase and walk away. An agent grabbed his arm and threw him against the car. Dave gasped and said, "Sorry for the confusion, but this doesn't have anything to do with me."

The agent stuck a .45-caliber pistol in Dave's mouth. "You move one more time, motherfucker, and I'll blow the back of your head off."

Dave tried to quell the toxic taste of steel and oil and discharged rounds, conscious of his knees giving way. While he sat handcuffed in the back of the car, he watched one of the agents open the briefcase Dave had carried, glance around, and quickly pocket what looked to be about $5,000.

Without speaking, they drove Eddie, Bob, and Dave to the Ventura County Jail.

* * *

A few blocks away on a relaxed drive to the same accounting meeting, Lou felt a rush of trepidation when he spotted a car following behind.

Trying to alter his course, he moved quickly through the tight turns, praying he would not hit a pedestrian or a runner, his heart clawing from his chest to his throat. *Do any streets in Santa Barbara follow a straight line?* Just like Eddie, Lou had not learned the area well enough or had become too comfortable in his security and impenetrability. The result: vulnerability. That's when he turned onto a road with only one outlet, right into a trap.

Lou sat still with his hands on the steering wheel as the men ran to his car and opened the driver's-side door, weapons drawn. One of them pushed a gun into Lou's cheek, hands trembling. Another said, "It's all over, Louie." Lou closed his eyes and exhaled methodically. The world began to spin, hurling random thoughts and memories through his consciousness. He saw himself in Cuba, then New York. Syracuse. College. Some law school. Then he saw 1963. He'd just heard about President Kennedy getting shot. As a young man in his twenties, concern for what he would do with his life, what would happen to his adopted country after this tragedy, gripped him. Then it was 1965, and he was teaching at Coronado High School. Helping students learn Spanish. Girls. Driving down to Tijuana in a crappy car for fifty bucks and enchiladas. Or were they tacos? Finding his artistry, his calling. What could he have done with a legitimate business? With a law degree? Women. Did he love them? Did it matter? Guarding his secrets. Keeping people close, but always on the outside. So many disguises—real and metaphorical—that he couldn't keep them straight. He could not differentiate reality from invention anymore. Maybe this agent with the gun was just another story. If so, why did the November sea breeze brushing the hot salt water escaping down one cheek feel so palpable? He reached up to wipe it away, but the men screamed at him to freeze. And he did, wondering how he could move around the country in luxury homes and hotels and cars, shuttling marijuana and millions of dollars in cash, staying hidden in this very large life for years—only to get caught driving to a meeting in a tony residential neighborhood.

When Lou opened his eyes, he knew this moment signaled the end of an era, the regrettable climax of who he was and could have been. Because he had chosen a path with such high switching costs, everything was forever altered.

Conklin, oddly serene at this pivotal juncture, told the more aggressive agents to back off, then escorted Lou back to his own house, in handcuffs, where agents interviewed the terrified sisters before sending them away. Lou had a feeling he would not see another woman for a very long time.

His mind churned as he listened to the agents slap high fives when they found what they called "bricks and bricks of high quality grass" in his basement. *Better than gold*, they said. And it was true. A decade in the business and he had never kept product in his house—until now. They threatened to blow up the massive safe, so he gave them the combination. Inside they found

$800,000 in cash, with envelopes prepared for paying the crew. Damning. And damned.

Lou pulled himself together and started thinking. He would not let this determine his fate. He would not go to jail. He wished he could talk to his psychic, but knew the smarter phone call would be to Phil DeMassa.

DEA agents transferred all four to the Metropolitan Correctional Center, or MCC, in San Diego. Bail for Lou and Eddie, the two leaders, was set at $5 million. Each.

A search of Bob's house, which agents labeled "the castle," yielded documents and payments to ships' captains. But they marveled most at the enormous closet that housed sixty-five pairs of shoes.

Later Conklin and his crew returned to Lou's house to finish the search and, for one night, sleep on the floor and the opium bed Lou used as a couch in the living room, because they had exceeded their budget for motels. When Conklin opened the refrigerator, he called out to his team: "Hey, we got no money for gas, but look at this." He hoisted a case of Heineken and started distributing the beer. "At least we won't go thirsty."

Another one yelled: "I was in the closet. Guy still has the tag on his designer jeans. Six hundred fifty bucks! What the *hell*!"

Conklin laughed. "Yep, we could all have our own rooms for the price of those pants!"

Basking in the seizures that could lead to the confiscation of property, cars, and cash worth millions of dollars, Conklin received yet another gift: a call from Lance Weber, who sounded a little crazy, possibly high, and extremely eager to become a confidential informant. He and Fuzzy preempted the fallout, asking to visit the DEA offices to share information in return for leniency. And protection. Lance, after all, understood what going to jail really meant. And he was ready to do and say anything to avoid returning. He would not sit around waiting to get caught. Plus, he reminded himself that he owed Lou and Eddie absolutely nothing.

What the DEA learned from Lance and Fuzzy would enable Conklin to issue additional indictments. In all, Conklin calculated that Lou, Eddie, Bob, and their cohorts had grossed more than $100 million through the 1970s and early '80s. To the agents the amount seemed astronomical, impossible.

But when Conklin suggested this to Lou, the former teacher smiled and thought: *Underestimated—again.*

Chapter 31

1982

LOU, EDDIE, BOB, AND DAVE RESIDED ON DIFFERENT floors at the MCC in San Diego for months, awaiting trial. The DEA investigated family members in Coronado and beyond, questioning friends who'd grabbed a beer with them, pressing women who'd partied or slept with them.

Lou and Eddie were convicted on multiple counts, including conspiracy to possess a controlled substance with intent to distribute, conspiracy to illegally import a controlled substance, and attempt to evade income tax.

Under Phil DeMassa's guidance, Lou withdrew a plea of not guilty and entered a plea of guilty. Eddie followed. The next month, they were each sentenced to a $40,000 fine and ten years in prison.

DeMassa outlined a strategy that took advantage of the shifting political landscape. Ronald Reagan was now the

President; many US Attorneys had changed with the new Republican leadership. This meant that a recent addition to the legal office might be willing to discuss ways to move some of the Company players off the books. DeMassa waited to see which players the authorities might consider trading.

Meanwhile, DeMassa hired private investigators Jack Palladino and Sandra Sutherland, a husband-and-wife team known for helping with the Patty Hearst kidnapping investigation in 1974, and an ongoing inquiry into the death of nine hundred members of a religious cult in Guyana in 1978. DeMassa wanted them to identify the confidential informant and dismantle the DEA's case, evidence, and tactics. He also began distributing money for safekeeping as fast as he could, following instructions that Lou issued from jail.

During one of his precious phone calls, Lou stood in his jumpsuit with his back against the wall so he could watch every move around him and said to DeMassa, "Who flipped on us?" Lou knew that Eddie remained steadfast. "The girls didn't know enough. The information could only come from Lance."

"Seems like Lance, but I have a couple of investigators trying to verify. We'll figure it out. Andy Willis's sloppiness didn't help."

"Lance is desperate. And nuts. If we prove who it is, will that give you leverage to pull it apart? Undermine him?" Lou sighed, his energy waning.

"Maybe."

"Listen, my friend. I don't know how many ways I can say

this, but I can't stay in jail." He lowered his voice. "Do anything. I don't care. Get me another hearing, and get me out of this place."

"You were facing forty-five years," DeMassa said evenly. "We agreed that you and Eddie would plead guilty and give up your property and cars for a reduced sentence. We did the best we could."

"No you didn't, Phil. You pushed me to take that terrible deal. You didn't pursue other options. Work on another plea. I'll testify against anyone."

"Even your former students, who care about you? Even Dave? Bob?"

Lou glanced around again, took a breath, and cupped a hand over the receiver. "Anyone."

"You know, Lou, they're going after me, too. The entire bar in San Diego hates me. But I'm just doing my job. Everyone deserves representation. Actually, I think they're jealous."

"Jesus, Phil. Save it. At least half a million dollars came from me. So I expect that you'll use it to get me the hell out of here."

"I'm trying, Lou."

"Because let me tell you: if someone has to do time, it won't be me."

Chapter 32

1982

LOU AND EDDIE WERE TRANSFERRED TO THE Federal Correctional Institution on Terminal Island—a terrifying block of cement on a man-made spit of land near Los Angeles. The island included a quarantine center, a Coast Guard base, a port for cargo ships, and more than eleven hundred prison inmates. Lou noted the irony of the address—1299 South Seaside Avenue in the beach community of San Pedro.

Eddie remained quiet, better prepared to serve time than the others because of the skills he'd honed over the previous eleven years. He'd fraternized and tumbled and brokered with criminals all over the world. And at twenty-eight years old, his perpetual smile exuded confidence, helped along by plenty of bulk and strength and a belief that everything in life came down to loyalty. He made friends, and spent any allotted free time lifting weights with them.

But jail terrified Lou, now in his forties. He sought refuge from the hostile environment by working in the library. His efforts to give up other Coronado Company members helped, but not enough. Lou's finely tuned negotiation skills told him that he needed to offer the Feds something they really wanted and could not get without his help.

With this realization, he saw only one remaining option: to trade his most valuable asset for his freedom, his sustenance. And that would mean turning on his attorney and consigliere, Phil DeMassa.

While Bob managed to get out on probation and engage in a successful stream of interlocutory appeals to delay his inevitable trial, Dave found himself at Boron Federal Prison in Death Valley. At one point he was transferred, in chains, to Terminal Island, where he saw a familiar face across the prison yard. He lifted his chin to Eddie, who left the clatter of the bench-press area and greeted Dave with a smile. "How you doin'?"

Dave's throat tightened and he fought back tears. "I've been better."

"Yeah, I know what you mean."

"What's happening? Where's Lou?"

"He's working on some deal, I heard. Got transferred down to the city jail in El Cajon to work with the DEA."

"Really?" Dave asked. "What kind of deal?"

"Not sure. But you know he'll roll over on everyone."

This thought made Dave nauseous. *How can Lou do this?*

"Lance and Fuzzy helped, I'm sure," Dave added.

"Everyone got pinched. And they're all cracking."

"What are you doing to get out?"

Eddie shrugged. "This is how it is. We screwed up, did one too many. Consequences, you know?"

"I can't do this, Eddie. I just . . . can't." Dave heard the despair in his own hollow voice.

"Hang in there, Dave. If you need any help, I'm here. I got your back, okay?"

"Thanks, Eddie." Dave mumbled. "That means a lot."

After a transfer to MCC (a gift when he learned that his cell-mate at Terminal Island had beheaded the previous bunkmate), Dave spent four months in solitary confinement, utterly alone for twenty-three hours a day. He requested legal textbooks, which he read until fatigue caused the print to blur. Each day provoked, plucked, and pulled at his tattered sanity.

He learned not to speak until spoken to; if you're the new guy, you keep your mouth shut. He fantasized about release and knew that if he ever faced the possibility of going back in, he would kill himself first. That would be far better than this torturous, slow death in a place that chipped away at his mental health with a dull chisel.

Dave tried not to turn on anyone in the Company. But he began to think that Lou was the smart one, and that his own approach lacked the valor he once assigned to it. Conklin knew this, and worked hard on Dave.

"You think this stuff is no big deal, right?" Conklin pushed.

"But I'm telling you, it's worse than you think. Kids lose motivation. Flunk out of school. Get addicted. And marijuana is a gateway drug to heroin, cocaine, LSD, amphetamines, opioids, everything else."

Dave stayed silent.

"You seem like a decent guy. And you always justified what you were doing, didn't you? No hard drugs, nobody got hurt, you paid what you owed, did business on a handshake. Like gentlemen."

Dave nodded.

"But did you think about what it does to young kids?"

Dave shook his head. "You're right."

"Okay, then. Let's get back to business. I know you don't want to hurt your buddies, but we visited you at Boron. We made offers that you rejected. This time, you need to help us—and by us, I mean the DEA, FBI, and IRS—or stay in jail for a very long time." Conklin paused for effect. "The train is leaving the station. You want to be on it, or under it?"

The federal government wielded a big stick in the form of the 848 statute, thickening the air with threats of the kingpin law for Dave, who was convinced he faced twenty years.

Every man was drowning, trying to save himself. Dave knew he would become demented or die if he spent another minute in prison. So he worked with Conklin to keep himself alive.

Eddie understood that he didn't have the book learning of Lou, Bob, and Dave, who had earned college degrees at good schools.

But Eddie also knew he made up for that in other ways. In the street world, breaking your word meant losing your business—or getting yourself killed. Eddie attributed his success to trusting the people closest to him, and his own reliability under threat. Others might call it foolish. But his survival depended on it.

On a sinking ship, maritime tradition says that a captain should make sure all his passengers evacuate safely before he abandons the vessel. Maybe Eddie had never been the only captain. But this ship was going down, and he could at least try to act like one.

In September Conklin received a call from former US Attorney Kevin McInerney, as respected in legal circles as Philip DeMassa was loathed. Lou Villar wanted to cooperate with the DEA because his previous attorney, Lou claimed, had not offered the opportunity to negotiate. In fact, Lou continued, Phil DeMassa had stolen from them and was actually *part of the conspiracy*. Did they want justice for this crooked attorney—who kept criminals far worse than lowly pot smugglers out of jail, year after year? Thankfully, Louis Villar could help.

So the court appointed McInerney to replace DeMassa. In return, Lou would also provide enough information to shut down other smugglers—for whom the Coronado Company ran off-loading gigs on occasion—and the Thai suppliers.

Conklin considered this. He was reluctant to give Lou a break. But his resources were dwindling. Lance—whom he called a "space cadet"—continued to offer information, yet it was clear he'd been out of the game for a while. Plus he and Fuzzy, still trying to keep their confidential informant status hidden from Lou and Eddie and Bob, wouldn't testify in a trial. So as abhorrent as it was for Conklin to consider striking a deal with a smuggler who could hide in a world of upscale businessmen, he liked the idea of going all the way to the suppliers. The legal community in San Diego also wanted nothing more than to remove Phil DeMassa from their club. It seemed like the prudent approach.

Conklin and his team met with Lou and Kevin McInerney over a period of several weeks, transporting Lou between the El Cajon jail and McInerney's office. Thrilled to be out of Terminal Island and on his way to freedom he could almost smell, Lou sat down in the reassuring surroundings of an elegant conference room, crossed his legs, sipped coffee, and shared with Conklin details of the past ten years.

Conklin used every bit of information Lou provided. Working together, the DEA and Federal prosecutors convicted sixty people related to the Coronado Company, arrested some of the Makah Indians at Neah Bay, helped court-martial the no-show helicopter pilots, and built a case against Phil DeMassa, with plenty of local support. In the coming years Conklin and his team worked with their foreign counterparts to seize $120 million worth of product, arrest major suppliers overseas, and systematically dismantle the Thai stick trade.

Chapter 33

1983–1984

AFTER BECOMING A GOVERNMENT WITNESS, LOU WAS resentenced for time served and extraordinary cooperation, and released from prison. The IRS absolved him of all fines. But Lou pushed for a few extras. These included the privilege to store his wine collection with an importer in San Diego, and to keep his most exotic furniture, $300,000 from the sale of the Hilton Head estate (minus the fee to the pesky Agnor brothers, of course), and his favorite Mercedes. He even managed to reduce the unsupervised probation. However, he remained at the mercy of the federal government.

With the information Lou supplied, Phil DeMassa faced twenty felony charges, including conspiracy to smuggle drugs, and, ironically, harboring a fugitive by keeping Bob Lahodny's house in his name. The DEA and IRS seized ninety-five boxes of files—250,000 documents—from DeMassa's office during an extended three-day raid.

Attorney Barry Tarlow represented DeMassa, maximizing every opportunity to speak to the press about government out of control. "Nothing like this has ever occurred in this country," he fumed on *Sixty Minutes*. "This is the most pervasive, the most intensive ransacking of a law office that has ever gone on in the United States. This search was an obscenity."

Lou filed a lawsuit, claiming that DeMassa had advised accepting an appalling plea bargain with a ten-year prison sentence. DeMassa, Lou continued, was protecting himself against information Lou could provide in a cooperative situation. Furthermore, DeMassa represented several Coronado Company members at the time and faced conflict-of-interest issues. The two used intermediaries and the press to spit at each other.

After eighteen months in prison and cooperation with Conklin and the federal government, Dave was released on a one-million-dollar bond, which his mother guaranteed with her Coronado Shores apartment. His marriage ended. So he stayed with his sister in San Diego and tried to find ways to reclaim his life. For a while he took accounting classes and enrolled in law school. But like Lou, he was at the mercy of the government, travelling to serve as a witness whenever the Feds demanded. It would take a long time before everything calmed down enough for him to feel remotely normal.

Even then, Dave knew his crimes would torment him—in job applications, social circles, and relationships—forever.

Chapter 34

1985–1986

FEARFUL OF THREATS ON HIS LIFE FROM FORMER suppliers, Lou changed his name, again, and disappeared, emerging only when he was summoned to testify. This included Bob Lahodny's trial in 1985. Bob had mastered delays and continuances enough to postpone his case for years. But when he found himself facing testimony from Lou, Dave, and Fuzzy, he decided to alter his plea to guilty and provide information. The agreement reduced his sentence to four years.

Phil DeMassa also went on trial in 1985. On the twenty-second day, before prosecutors called Lou Villar to the stand, DeMassa deftly navigated the system he knew so well. He entered a guilty plea to four lesser charges, including illegal currency transactions and harboring fugitives. This gave authorities little else to pursue. It also left Lou looking foolish if he chose to continue engaging in the public brawl, played out in the media, where the two men called each other "manipulative" and "exploitative" as they battled over $320,000 in proceeds from a condo in South Carolina after the government seized and sold it.

Facing twenty years, Philip DeMassa was sentenced in December 1985 to six months in the New Horizons halfway house for his role in the Coronado Company. Probation officers had recommended a three-year prison sentence and a fine of $100,000, which DeMassa agreed to pay (with money he had stolen from Lou and Dave, they insisted) as part of the plea bargain.

"I think it's refreshing that the judge took an independent view of the case, made a fair sentence, and didn't succumb to the lies and misrepresentation of the government," DeMassa told reporters. Beginning in February 1986, he breezed through a sentence that lasted only four and a half months.

Because he did not plead guilty to crimes involving moral turpitude, his license to practice law would be suspended, but not revoked—a lenient outcome the legal community in San Diego would condemn for decades. The next year, in 1986, Lou Villar ended his five-year battle with Phil DeMassa by dropping the malpractice lawsuit against his former defense attorney and settling into a quiet, law-abiding, taxpaying life. For a while, he became a personal trainer.

No contact occurred between Lou and Dave until each was subpoenaed to testify for a grand jury in Maine. When Dave spotted Lou and Fuzzy on the same flight, he seethed and swore to himself that he would not speak to his former mentor. The anger felt as fresh and raw as if the betrayal had occurred the week before.

But during the flight, Lou and Dave started chatting. Then over a lobster dinner and lubricating drinks in Bar Harbor with their federal agent hosts, the three men managed to start laughing. Lou convinced Dave that he was merely trying to get out from underneath what had happened. He didn't want to hurt anyone, didn't want to tell their story. But after Andrew Willis and Phil DeMassa had ripped them off, and everyone had testified against them, he'd had no choice. He was a businessman, after all, a survivor. He'd suffered from his choices, and run out of options, just like everyone else.

Over the course of the evening, they realized that in their new lives, nobody could comprehend them the way they knew and understood each other's flaws, deceptions, and desires. Without saying anything about their friendship, they knew it would endure while they grappled with the adjustment to conventional life. Both, they were sure, would continue until they died.

Chapter 35

1989–2002

BOB LAHODNY FINISHED SERVING FOUR YEARS IN prison in 1989, not long after Eddie was released from Terminal Island and moved to Rimini Road in Del Mar—one of the assets he had managed to retain by keeping his name away from it. The two old friends reconnected over beers and stories reaching back to their Coronado days, riding bikes around town as they planned the adventures that would become their lives. The conversation turned to prison and the current struggle to figure out what they would do next, how they would transition to nine-to-five jobs after what they'd experienced.

"The most regular job I ever worked was lifeguarding!" Eddie blurted.

"Yeah, I can't say that sailing around the South Pacific was much of a job," Bob added.

They drifted for weeks, months. Eddie threw a thirty-fifth

birthday party for himself by his pool, mixed a few bowls of his punch, turned up Sting singing with the Police, and pulled Bob aside.

"You know Frank Cooney, right?" Eddie said.

"Sure. He was in my class. Good guy."

"Says he needs my help. Wants to know if we could do another load. He's got a sick kid, or something. Can't afford to pay the medical bills."

"Really? I heard he got arrested."

"Nah, he's just trying to be a good dad."

"Doesn't sound right. How much are you thinking?"

Eddie shrugged. "Just like we used to. But it's gotta be worth it."

"Eddie, look what you have here. Gorgeous house. Independence. You sure about this?"

Eddie laughed. No, he wasn't certain about anything. He had already served jail time. Years. Ironically, paying his dues made launching life on the outside incredibly difficult. The Feds had snatched most of his money; adjusting his lifestyle proved more challenging than he had anticipated. He'd been dabbling, but if he arranged one more load, he could help Frank's daughter, and still have enough to start his own business. Later.

First he would go back to the beginning and work on details that he could recite in his sleep: suppliers in Mexico (Special Agent Jim Conklin's disruption of the Thai trade forced Eddie to go south), a vessel to carry the product, Zodiacs, wet suits, tide charts, trucks, two-way radios, a lean crew, key distributors.

They could keep it simple and safe, and break the tedium of their current existence. He just felt so . . . restless. And lost.

Eddie sipped the punch, feeling it burn the back of his throat. Bob watched him, saying nothing. After all these years, they didn't really need to speak. Over the next few minutes Eddie didn't so much decide as gravitate toward something comforting and familiar, something he did well and missed.

He cocked his head and grinned. "What the hell else am I going to do?"

"You're on your own for this one. I have my own thing brewing." Bob raised his glass. "But I wish you well."

Eddie clinked his glass against Bob's. "One more time."

In early March, Eddie offered Frank Cooney a position on the crew, with payment of $35,000. He included extra money to buy a wet suit and a torch to cut through a locked gate to a quiet area with less foot traffic. They would off-load there.

On March 31, Eddie left Rimini Road in his black Nissan pickup truck. In the bed underneath the fiberglass camper shell were two eighteen-foot rubber rafts, two outboard motors, food, water, and beer. On April 1, Eddie rented U-Haul trucks in Santa Rosa.

The next day Frank Cooney introduced Eddie to a guy who wanted to become part of the crew. They needed help. Eddie trusted Frank, so he offered the new recruit $10,000.

The crew drove to Rockport, California, about two hundred miles north of San Francisco and less than forty miles south of

Sinkyone Wilderness State Park and the Lost Coast Dave had discovered for the Company more than a decade earlier. Eddie set up a stash location to repackage, shrink-wrap, box, and distribute in a nearby town called Leggett.

At about nine fifteen p.m. Eddie and his crew backed two U-Haul trucks toward the water, unloaded their own gear and provisions to take to the ship—including food, motor oil, and a few cases of beer for goodwill—and used strobe lights and two-way radios to communicate with the vessel.

Eddie heard the captain's voice. But the Coast Guard intercepted the communication and responded. Eddie shut off the radio and watched through his night-vision binoculars.

He saw and heard nothing but stillness.

When Eddie's watch passed midnight, his stomach churned. He couldn't wait anymore. "Get out there!" he yelled to the beach crew, forgetting the volume of his voice. "Head west. Find that goddamn ship before it leaves! And no radios." He found himself impatient with their inability to do what he'd managed in half the time as a seventeen-year-old. "Come on, move it!"

They pushed the Zodiac onto the dark water. *Ten tons*, Eddie thought, sweat breaking out on his forehead, despite the chill in the Northern California air. *Please don't leave with ten fucking tons of weed.*

When the contractors returned empty-handed after circling the area for over an hour, Eddie cursed. He should have gone out himself. These were not his Coronado Company teammates, not Fuzzy and Don operating with meticulous planning from Dave, seamless instruction from Lou, and distant support from an eternally calm Bob. He hated to admit that he missed those guys, the camaraderie, "hanging out with people on the same wavelength," as Fuzzy once said. He missed people who understood everything before it happened, who knew what you were thinking and feeling even when you didn't.

Years in prison had kept Eddie on high alert. But he also hated to admit that he was rusty at frontline activity. In fact, he'd never possessed a knack for the details like Dave. He thought he'd done a decent job putting it all together. But when it all hit the fan, he realized, plan B or C didn't exist.

By two a.m. Eddie ordered everyone to reload and depart for Leggett. As he drove northeast on Highway 1 just before dawn on April 3, authorities surrounded Eddie's truck, just as they had his Mercedes in Santa Barbara—at a moment when he least expected it, after a failed delivery.

Every part of him went numb. He closed his eyes and tightened his abs, bracing for impact. Then he gathered his resolve to accept, and endure, the ramifications. They would be steep and sharp.

Armed with a search warrant for Eddie's house in Del Mar, authorities found another two-way radio and the most essential information of all (to Eddie): a tide chart for the San Francisco Bay area. With logs from the confidential informants Eddie had trusted, the DEA had everything it needed.

Bail was not allowed due to "risk of flight." Charged with

conspiracy to import marijuana, Eddie entered a plea of not guilty on April 11, 1989, and was sentenced to ten years in prison. Handcuffs, chains, jumpsuit, good-byes.

His best friend was not far away. At about this time, authorities arrested Bob Lahodny on unrelated drug charges, alleging that he had participated in a deal to sell eleven pounds of cocaine. He, too, would return to jail.

In 1991 Dave married his high school girlfriend. That December, he sent a holiday card to Superior Court Judge Ray Edwards, who, as Assistant US Attorney, had helped prosecute Dave, Eddie, Lou, and Bob. Dave wrote that while his law school studies remained unfinished, he had launched a respectable career, and was "now a family man again. (Feels right.)"

Years passed. One day, back at the MCC, inmate Eddie Otero watched an unruly scene erupt. Another prisoner managed to obtain a shank and use it to hold a guard hostage, resulting in an ongoing siege that kept the prisoners from their meals and other small privileges of great importance in their daily routines. Eddie crept behind the captor, restrained him in a headlock, and wrestled away the scrap-metal-turned-homemade-knife. "Listen, buddy," Eddie hissed. "We're not getting fed. So you're gonna take this shit somewhere else."

Prison guards descended on Eddie, pinning him to the ground and screaming until the one who had been attacked regained his voice enough to explain that Ed Otero had, in fact, saved his life.

The heroics facilitated Eddie's release two years early, just before Christmas in 1997.

He vowed never to go back.

At forty-three years old, Eddie decided to start his new life with friends and drinks and AC/DC bellowing "You Shook Me All Night Long" at a belated fortieth birthday party. Later he moved to Palm Springs and built a legitimate—and successful—water and air purification business, based on ozone technology he developed.

In 2001 he met and married Desiree. He told his friends he had found the love of his very full life. They bought a sailing boat, traveled, gardened, and ran the company together. On a pottery wheel in their backyard, he taught her ceramics. Eddie satisfied his thrill-seeking compulsions with deep-sea fishing expeditions in Mexico and the ups and downs of his cherished San Diego Padres and Chargers.

Eventually he circled back to Coronado and his lifeguarding mentor; the Admiral was also an elementary school teacher who had arranged for his students to write letters to Eddie in jail. But for all of the Admiral's affection, he never let Eddie off the hook, saying, "Hey, yeah, those are the choices you made."

Eddie didn't make excuses or deflect blame. He learned plenty of lessons in jail, or "charm school," as he liked to call it, and said without equivocation, "I'm done."

After a morning visit with his parents in their condominium near Sacred Heart, Eddie retraced the commute of his youth. At the corner where Seventh Street meets D Avenue, he stood in front of Coronado High School for the first time in thirty years.

Students strolled onto campus talking over each other about homework, teachers, gossip, *American Idol*, parties, Usher, Joey and George and *Friends* and *ER*, moving around Eddie as if he were just another adult they needed to ignore. Something kept him rooted to that patch of sidewalk as a montage of recollections barged into his consciousness: the ripple of the water polo cage net when he scored a goal. Tumbling through surf with fifty pounds tied to his ankle. Dave's laughter when a delivery succeeded. The sound of his breathing during a rescue. Orange stains over the jetty at sunset. The comforting thrum of a pottery wheel in motion. Cruising on a bicycle, hands free, next to Bob. Exhaust fumes and gun barrels on a clear November day in Santa Barbara. The obvious and hidden horrors of prison. Lou Villar emerging from his Corvette with a smile and a word of encouragement.

Thoughts of Lou broke the trance. It wasn't Eddie's style to dwell; living in the moment was the only way to endure prison, after all. But the breach of trust from someone he admired so much, someone who'd been part of his family, still hurt.

Eddie turned away from the school and began walking toward the beach, the burden of his past inescapable. So many crimes. And so many more repercussions.

But when he looked back on his exhilarating life, at least he could feel good about one thing: he always kept his word.

EPILOGUE

JAMES (JIM) CONKLIN RETIRED FROM THE DEA AND runs a private investigation agency in Las Vegas, Nevada.

Robert (Bobby) Dunne retired from the DEA, and lives in the Northwest with his wife.

Dennis (Denny) Grimaud retired from the Coronado Police Department, and lives in Coronado with his wife.

Philip (Phil) DeMassa died in 2012 following a diving accident in the ocean off Hawaii Kai on Oahu, Hawaii. He was sixty-seven.

Al Sweeney moved back to Coronado, and died in 1985.

Allan (Fuzzy) Maguire (not his real name) works and lives in an undisclosed location.

Don Kidd still shares his mechanical expertise—for a price—in Oregon.

Paul Acree's whereabouts are unknown.

Lance Weber died in Coronado in 2000, at age fifty-six, from amyotrophic lateral sclerosis (ALS).

Robert (Bob) Lahodny retired to La Jolla, and died just

before his sixty-first birthday in 2010 from complications of hepatitis C.

David (Dave) Stratton (not his real name) lives with his wife in an undisclosed location.

Edward (Eddie) Otero died in 2013 while fishing off the coast of Mexico. He was fifty-nine.

Louis (Lou) Henry Villar lives in an undisclosed location under an assumed name. In early 2017, he turned eighty.

ACKNOWLEDGMENTS

Many thanks go to the people who made this book possible, most notably my agent, Laura Gross, for her friendship and belief in my writing. To my editor, Fiona Simpson, for seeing enough potential in my fictionalized account of the Coronado Company to assign the real thing. And to Brian Luster and everyone at Simon & Schuster who worked on this book behind the scenes.

I also owe my gratitude to those who experienced different facets of this story and were willing to share their memories, insights, and connections in repeated interviews, including but not limited to Larry Cartwright, Jim Conklin, Joe Ditler, Robert Dunne, Judge Ray Edwards, Russ Elwell, Dennis Grimaud, Candice Hooper, Peter Núñez, Desiree Otero, Judge Christine Pate, Judge William Pate, Pike Meade, Pamela Murphy Moreno, George Murphy, Patrick Murphy, Jerry Vickers, Sandra Vickers, and of course some members of the Coronado Company.

It's impossible to write a book about Coronado without acknowledging the remarkable teachers at Coronado Middle School and High School, whose dedication motivates me still: Robin Adair, George Arnall, Pat Bennett, Kathy Clark, Sandy Ferguson, Ron Jones, Roy Matthews, Kathleen Snow, Don Valliere, and many others.

I can't offer enough thanks to my Yale School of Management classmates and dear friends, who helped me balance the writing and release of a book with staggering amounts of homework. I especially want to thank Sunil Eappen for listening to me read aloud and offering feedback during our commutes. I'm also indebted to the professors, including my advisor Nathan Novemsky. They challenged me to think differently about the world, and helped me understand the humor, tragedy, and humanity in this story of entrepreneurialism run afoul.

I would like to thank my family and friends, particularly my mother, Sandra, for sharing the wisdom of her six decades in Coronado and for encouraging me to write, and my father, Peter, for the sense of purpose that transcends his death; my stepparents, Jerry and Betsy, for their unfailing advocacy; my husband, David, who waded through the first draft and supported me along the entire process; Rosie Zweiback, my former teaching colleague and longtime friend, who edited the earliest attempts at the fictionalized version that helped get me here; and the faithful friends who have sustained me with meaningful relationships over the years.

My deepest appreciation goes to my children, Christopher and Alison, for inspiring me with their patience and love as they watched me (sometimes from under a newsroom desk) pursue a career that often meant working on deadline in a cubicle, almost entirely devoid of the glamour anyone might vaguely associate with becoming a writer. This perseverance is for them.

SOURCES

Interviews

Larry Cartwright, James Conklin, Joseph Ditler, Robert Dunne, Judge Raymond Edwards, Russell (the Admiral) Elwell, Dennis Grimaud, Pike Meade, Pamela Murphy Moreno, George Murphy, Patrick Murphy, Peter Núñez, Desiree Otero, Jerry Vickers, Sandra Vickers, and many others who asked to remain anonymous

Other Sources

Coronado High School Library

Coronado Public Library

Coronado Historical Association

National Archives

Bearman, Joshuah. "Coronado High." *The Atavist,* https://magazine.atavist.com/coronado-high.

Bearman, Joshuah. "Coronado High: A Legendary Drug-Smuggling Ring in a Sleepy California Town." *GQ,* September 8, 2013, http://www.gq.com/story/joshuah-bearman-argo-coronado-company-drug-smuggling-ring.

Carlin, Katherine Eitzen and Ray Brandes. *Coronado: The Enchanted Island, Fourth Edition.* Coronado, CA: Coronado Historical Association, 2015.

SOURCES

Copperwaite, Paul, ed. *The Mammoth Book of Drug Barons*. Philadelphia: Running Press, 2010.

"The Coronado Mob." *Sixty Minutes*, https://www.youtube.com/watch?v=K18hJj-Xja8.

Court Records, United States District Court, Southern District of California

- US v. Otero (Judge Enright), CR-89-00351-01

- US v. Lahodny (Judge Keep), CR-83-789-K

- US v. Weber, CR-77-00896-02

"Drug Enforcement Administration: 1970–1975," http://www.dea.gov/about/history/1970-1975.pdf.

Holbreich, Curt. "2 Members of Drug Ring Seized Again." *Los Angeles Times*, April 5, 1989. http://articles.latimes.com/1989-04-05/local/me-830_1_san-diego.

"Louis Villar sentenced for drug distribution." *Coronado Eagle and Journal*, February 11, 1982. http://cdnc.ucr.edu/cgi-bin/cdnc?a=d&d=CJ19820211.2.10.

Maguire, Peter and Mike Ritter. *Thai Stick: Surfers, Scammers, and the Untold Story of the Marijuana Trade*. New York: Columbia University Press, 2013.

Martino, Michael T. *Images of America: Lifeguards of San Diego County*. Charleston, SC: Arcadia Publishing, 2007.

Report of Investigation from DEA, Operation CorCo

- Debriefing of CI SR2820045 (Louis Villar), September 22, 1982

- Affidavit: DEA, Northern District of California

Reza, H. G. "Controversy Still Lingers as DeMassa Trial Readied." *Los Angeles Times*, October 8, 1985. http://articles.latimes.com/1985-10-08/local/me-15333_1_fair-trial.

276

Schachter, Jim. "Coronado Co. Lawyer: DeMassa Sentenced to 6 Months in Drug Case." *Los Angeles Times*, December 31, 1985. http://articles.latimes.com/1985-12-31/local/me-26448_1_drug-case.

Schachter, Jim. "DeMassa, Villar Bury Hatchet in Secret Deal." *Los Angeles Times*, July 26, 1986. http://articles.latimes.com/1986-07-26/local/me-153_1_malpractice-suit.

Survivors Benefit Fund. "Ralph N. Shaw." https://www.survivorsbenefitfund.org/?fuseaction=woh.show&key=4a71caad-5b72-4363-920c-e42f4d538619.

United States Census Bureau

Department of Industrial Relations, State of California: http://www.dir.ca.gov/iwc/minimumwagehistory.htm.

ABOUT THE AUTHOR

Katherine Nichols is a former teacher and longtime journalist who has contributed to numerous publications, including the magazines for the *New York Times* and *San Francisco Chronicle*. An athlete since childhood, Katherine is a three-time finisher of the IRONMAN World Championship in Hawaii. She grew up in Coronado and lives in Boston.